The Literature of Cinema

THE LITERATURE OF CINEMA presents
a comprehensive selection from the multitude
of writings about cinema, rediscovering materials on its origins, history, theoretical prin-
ciples and techniques, aesthetics, economics,
and effects on societies and individuals. Included are works of inherent, lasting merit
and others of primarily historical significance.
These provide essential resources for serious
study and critical enjoyment of the "magic
shadows" that became one of the decisive cul-
tural forces of modern times.

Children's Attendance At Motion Pictures

Edgar Dale

The Emotional Responses of Children to the Motion Picture Situation

Wendell S. Dysinger and Christian A. Ruckmick

ARNO PRESS & THE NEW YORK TIMES

New York • 1970

109/07

Reprint Edition 1970 by Arno Press Inc.
Library of Congress Catalog Card Number: 75-125462
ISBN 0-405-01643-3
ISBN for complete set: 0-405-01600-X
Manufactured in the United States of America

CHILDREN'S ATTENDANCE
AT MOTION PICTURES

BY

EDGAR DALE

RESEARCH ASSOCIATE, BUREAU OF EDUCATIONAL RESEARCH
OHIO STATE UNIVERSITY

NEW YORK
THE MACMILLAN COMPANY
1935

THIS SERIES OF TWELVE STUDIES OF THE
INFLUENCE OF MOTION PICTURES UPON
CHILDREN AND YOUTH HAS BEEN MADE BY
THE COMMITTEE ON EDUCATIONAL RE-
SEARCH OF THE PAYNE FUND AT THE RE-
QUEST OF THE NATIONAL COMMITTEE FOR
THE STUDY OF SOCIAL VALUES IN MOTION
PICTURES, NOW THE MOTION PICTURE RE-
SEARCH COUNCIL, 366 MADISON AVENUE,
NEW YORK CITY. THE STUDIES WERE DE-
SIGNED TO SECURE AUTHORITATIVE AND
IMPERSONAL DATA WHICH WOULD MAKE
POSSIBLE A MORE COMPLETE EVALUATION
OF MOTION PICTURES AND THEIR SOCIAL
POTENTIALITIES

ACKNOWLEDGMENTS

Acknowledgments are made to the following persons:

To Mr. James LaPoe, who visited approximately one half of the centers where the study was carried out, and who gave assistance during the early part of the investigation.

To Miss Elva Lyon, who had charge of the statistical work of the investigation.

To Dr. Mary Mark and Miss Eleanor Morris, who were responsible for securing the data presented in Chapter VII.

To Miss Hazel Gibbony, Mrs. Walter Howe, and Mr. Louis E. Raths of the Bureau of Educational Research, who assisted in the preparation of the manuscript.

TABLE OF CONTENTS

v

LIST OF TABLES

vii

LIST OF CHARTS

ATTENDANCE AT MOTION PICTURES

CHAPTER I

FINDINGS OF THE STUDY

THE major aim of this study was to discover the frequency of attendance of school children at commercial motion pictures in relation to age, sex, companions, time of day, day of attendance, and program offerings most frequently viewed. The study was conducted during the year 1929–1930.

Answers to the following questions were sought:

1. How frequently do children of different ages attend motion pictures?
2. Are some nights or days loaded more heavily than others, or is the attendance about the same every day?
3. Do young children go as frequently in the evening as older children?
4. Who accompanies these children to the movies?
5. How long do children stay at the pictures?
6. What feature of the program is most popular with children?
7. To what extent can the child's own statement of attendance be relied upon?

The facts were secured in two ways. First, observers stationed near the ticket-taker in theaters noted the proportion of the audience which was composed of persons under the age of seven, from seven to thirteen, from fourteen to twenty, and twenty-one and over. The city of

Columbus, Ohio, was used for this study. For approximately three months a group of observers systematically checked the attendance at fifteen Columbus theaters. This number represented a sampling of about one third of the theaters, and each type of theater was appropriately represented. Each theater was checked for a week. The composition of the Columbus movie audience was as follows:

Under 7	2.8 per cent
7–13	11.8 per cent
14–20	22.1 per cent
21 or more	63.3 per cent

These figures, if applied to the country as a whole, probably represent a minimum, for these reasons: The percentage of population under fifteen in Columbus is 23.1, in Ohio 27.4, and in the United States 29.4 (1930 census). Of the 21 Ohio cities having more than 25,000 inhabitants, Columbus ranks eighteenth in percentage of children under the age of fifteen. Lakewood, Cincinnati, and East Cleveland are the only Ohio cities over 25,000 in population which have lower proportions of children under fifteen than has Columbus. Cleveland, Pittsburgh, New York, Chicago, Philadelphia, Baltimore, Boston, and Detroit all have higher percentages of children under fifteen years of age than Columbus. Los Angeles and St. Louis are the only extremely large cities which have fewer children under fifteen than has Columbus. We see, therefore, that our data regarding the percentage of children in motion-picture theaters probably lead to an underestimate for the country at large. So we are safe in concluding that more than one third of the motion-picture audiences throughout the United States are composed of children and youth under the age of twenty-one.

A second method was the use of an inquiry blank from

which we secured attendance data on approximately 55,000 children from the kindergarten through the twelfth grade in fifty different communities in Ohio and several different communities in one other state. We discovered that in a seven-day period 16,750 Ohio boys and girls in the primary grades attended 7,008 times or an average of .42 times a week. The 35,453 boys and girls in grades 4 to 12 attended 35,155 times or an average (mean) of almost exactly one attendance a week. Twenty-two per cent of the group in the primary grades reported to their teacher that they never attend.

The most popular days for motion-picture attendance by children are, in order of popularity, Saturday, Sunday, Friday, Wednesday, Monday, Tuesday, and Thursday. About one third of all the attendances were on Saturday, one fourth on Sunday, and one eighth on Friday. Almost three fourths of the attendances, therefore, are concentrated on the week-end.

If the popularity of the feature picture, newsreel, and comedy can be judged properly by the frequency with which each is viewed more than once, the main picture, the newsreel, and the comedy can be compared by these data. If the child had viewed each feature only once, the average (mean) in each case would be represented by the figure 1.

Feature	Mean Attendances		
	Boys	Girls	Both
Main picture	1.22	1.19	1.21
Newsreel	1.22	1.15	1.19
Comedy	1.31	1.22	1.26

Boys spend more time in the movies than girls. Both groups spend more time viewing the comedy than either of the other two features of the program. The time spent in re-viewing these three features becomes less with increasing maturity.

The companions of children at the movies are distributed in percentages as follows:

	Boys	Girls	Both
Father	2.63	2.63	2.63
Mother	3.65	9.13	6.13
Father and mother	6.37	9.83	7.94
Brother or sister	14.81	18.99	16.70
Own friends	34.77	35.77	35.22
Some one else	11.48	14.77	12.96
No companion	25.18	7.89	17.37
No data	1.10	.98	1.05

Girls are accompanied by their parents almost twice as often as boys. Of the total attendances for both boys and girls, 16.7 per cent are with brother or sister as companions. More children go with their own friends than with any other group. Three times as many boys go alone to the movies as girls.

The time of day when boys and girls from the age of eight to nineteen attend is as follows:

	Boys	Girls	Both
Morning	2.90	2.41	2.68
Afternoon	30.02	33.15	31.43
Evening	67.08	64.44	65.89

The morning attendance is indeed slight (less than 3 per cent). About one third of the attendance is in the afternoon and two thirds in the evening. There is a tendency for girls to go more frequently in the afternoon than the boys and less frequently in the evening. The difference between boys and girls in morning attendance is slight.

Finally, it can be stated that almost all children everywhere are being directly exposed to motion pictures which are shown at commercial theaters. The only ones who escape its influence are the very young and those who live in areas where inaccessibility of the theater makes it physically impossible to attend. This fact of universal exposure is proved. Proof of the effect of the exposure is left to other contributors in this series of volumes.

The following chapters will discuss in more detail the findings of the study, the techniques used, the adequacy of the techniques, and the inferences to be drawn from the data.

CHAPTER II

THE MOTION–PICTURE PROBLEM

PARENTS, educators, and others are growing exceedingly critical of those agencies which form the characters of children. They are anxious to know which of these agencies are beneficial and which are harmful to character. Unfortunately the data by which one might arrive at sound inferences are alarmingly meager. This lack of data has two causes: first, the absence until just recently of a desire for scientific and factual data in this area; and second, the practical and scientific difficulties faced by those desirous of carrying on research in this field.

Although the concern for character education is not a new one, nevertheless parents and educators of other days were not faced with a problem so baffling and of such magnitude as that found today. In earlier times it was far easier to note the causes of various kinds of behavior and to check the effects of training. People led restricted lives, necessarily so because of the heavy burden of securing the bare necessities of life, and leisure time was indeed limited. Further, if misconduct was discovered among children the number of agencies which might have caused that behavior were few in number. Behavior was in large measure influenced by direct experiences in one's environment. Indirect experiences were limited almost entirely to those which passed by word of mouth or through the few reading materials available.

Contrast this situation with the one which now prevails. Today our modes of transportation have greatly increased the possibilities of direct contact with a wide variety of experience, and the radio, the press, and motion pictures have multiplied almost infinitely the possibilities of indirect contacts. In earlier times a behavior consequence could be fairly easily connected with its antecedents because there were few variables to be considered. Today, however, such a consequence is often preceded by a puzzling variety of antecedents. As a result, one of the major scientific labors of this and many generations to come will be to note the various antecedent variables suspected as the cause of specific types of behavior, to analyze these data, and then to discover the antecedent, accompanying, and consequent correlates of these variables.

One of these behavior-producing mechanisms over which a great deal of concern is being felt is the motion picture. At least two major methods of research are available for the study of the influence of motion pictures on human behavior. First, we may study the behavior of wide groups of children and note what differences in behavior are found among those who attend motion pictures frequently and those who attend rarely. This is a statistical approach and it necessitates a wide amount of accurate information concerning the children or adults who are studied. Among other things, an exact measure of their motion-picture attendance is imperative. The second approach is the experimental one. Two groups of children equal in all important respects are selected; one group is subjected to certain motion-picture experiences, and the effects noted. Here we are interested in attendance only from the standpoint of seeing that antecedent experiences of children in reference to motion pictures are equal. In both types of experiments, however, it becomes exceedingly critical that accurate attendance data be secured.

The usefulness of attendance data. In what ways can attendance data secured from a large sampling of children all over the United States be utilized in solving some of the behavior problems suggested above? Let us suppose that we have discovered certain favorable behavior attitudes among children. We wish now to discover what agencies coöperated in causing these results. If these benefits are widespread among all children, then certainty that motion pictures are the single cause must rest upon the discovery that motion-picture attendance is a widespread activity of children in all parts of the country, and that the peculiar type of behavior under study always has motion-picture attendance and no other variable as a constant antecedent. This same type of data can be utilized when distinct forms of undesirable behavior are discovered.

A second possible use of such data lies in its value when the case for children's films is presented. Through the data that they have presented relative to children's attendance, the motion-picture producers have attempted to deny the importance of children as a factor in economic benefits to them through child attendance at motion pictures. This is illustrated by the following statement:

> Incidentally, the absurd statement has been made that 75 per cent of our motion picture audiences is made up of children. As a matter of fact only eight per cent are children.[1]

Statements such as these have commonly been used by motion-picture producers as an argument against making films for children. On the other hand, astute motion-picture producers themselves have been on the alert to keep children in the motion-picture houses. This is especially well

[1] Will H. Hays in "Supervision from Within," from *The Story of the Films,* Harvard Graduate School of Business Administration, 1927.

indicated by the following statement of Jesse L. Lasky in the 1931 *Film Daily Year Book of Motion Pictures.* He says:

A return to the technique of the old silent pictures, together with the vastly improved sound achieved by the new "noiseless-recording" system and the concerted drive to bring the children back to the theater, will show results this year.[2]

The *Film Daily* of April 15, 1931, acknowledges very frankly that child attendance at motion pictures has been below the usual amount during the time when the study reported in this monograph was made:

Now that a definite trend has been established in bringing the youngsters back to the pictures, it might not be out of order to suggest the charting of a straight course in regard to these regular patrons of tomorrow. Wide-awake exhibitors appreciate and will not again risk the loss of juvenile patronage. We find them offering special Kid Matinées and Saturday morning performances. Adjusting their admission prices for youngsters. Forming "Kiddie Clubs." Giving souvenirs to children. Having a "Kid" page in their program. Conducting contests in schools and making their houses more attractive to the younger generation in many ways. As a matter of established domestic record, our own picture-minded youngsters take us, nine times out of ten, to the pictures of their choice. So do millions of others.

The evidence presented above indicates that there has been misrepresentation by motion-picture organizations of the amount of child attendance, that the producers have "viewed with alarm" the exodus of children from motion-picture theaters, and that they are bending every effort to get them to return. This suggests very strongly that the children are wanted and that the exhibitors are anxious to learn how to keep them attending motion pictures.

[2] P. 550.

It is the purpose of this study to get at the facts of child attendance. This is done in three different ways. First, the studies previously made in the field are presented; second, a technique for measuring attendance was developed; and third, this technique of measurement was applied to approximately 55,000 children.

CHAPTER III
TECHNIQUES USED IN THE INVESTIGATION OF THE MOTION–PICTURE HABITS OF SCHOOL CHILDREN

THIS chapter is concerned with attendance data gathered directly from school children. Two types of blanks were used for this purpose (see Appendix I). The inquiry blank shown as Inquiry Blank A was used to gather information directly from children in grades four through twelve. Inquiry Blank B was used for the kindergarten and grades one, two, and three. The children in this latter group who were able to write satisfactorily kept a diary record for one week of their motion-picture attendance. The teacher secured attendance information from the very young children by means of an interview.

The validity of the information secured in this fashion was checked in various ways. In a study made at Collinwood High School in Cleveland, Ohio, we found that when we had one half of the children sign their names and one half of them remain anonymous, there was no difference whatsoever in the average (mean) attendance score. This indicated very clearly that there was no attempt on the part of the child to withhold or distort facts concerning his motion-picture attendance.

A second check on validity was obtained by having children fill out an attendance questionnaire and then write reviews of the pictures which they saw that week. The evidence indicated that there was a close agreement between the number of satisfactory reviews written and the number of pictures which the child had reported on the questionnaire.

11

A third check for validity was the interviewing during
the summer of 1930 of 252 children between the ages of
nine and fourteen. These children were interviewed on
either Monday, Tuesday, or Wednesday and were asked
questions regarding their movie attendance of the previous week. That children remember the frequency of attendance, the day on which they attended, what they saw, and
the name of the picture is indicated by the following data:

> Only one child could not remember whether he had gone once
> or twice.
> Only two gave the wrong day.
> Six could not remember what they saw.
> One could remember only the comedy and not the feature.

The validity in the case of these interviews was checked
in this manner: If a child said that he went to the Garden
Theater on Friday and saw Ramon Novarro in "The Call
of the Flesh," the investigator merely looked at a chart
which showed all pictures appearing in Columbus during
the past week. In this way discrepancies were easily de-
tected when they occurred.

Some of the reasons why children are able to remember
this type of data are as follows:

> a. They may be regularly attending a serial which appears once
> a week on a specified night.
> b. Almost three fourths of the attendances of children are con-
> centrated in the week-end. Thus for most children the
> problem of validity is one of the accuracy of their memory
> of an event two or three days after the event has occurred.

The communities studied. A careful attempt was made to
study all types of communities in which varying attendance might be found. The sampling was so adjusted that
industrial, commercial, suburban, and rural areas of various
kinds in different parts of the state of Ohio would be in-

cluded. That the state was well sampled geographically is
indicated by the map (see Appendix II). An alphabetized list
of the Ohio cities and districts studied follows. (All towns
not otherwise indicated have complete reports from the
primary through grade twelve.)

1. Adena (grades 4–8, 10, 11)
2. Akron
3. Belle Center (grades 1–8)
4. Bexley (ages 6–14)
5. Bowling Green
6. Bucyrus
7. Cadiz
8. Chardon
9. Cleveland (Collinwood—junior and senior high school)
10. Columbus (North High—senior high school)
11. Crestline
12. Dayton
13. De Graff
14. Dunkirk
15. Fremont
16. Gallipolis
17. Greenfield
18. Greenville
19. Grandview
20. Jackson
21. Johnstown
22. Kinsman
23. Lakeview
24. Lima
25. Logan County (grades 1–8)
26. Marietta
27. Middletown (no primary) [1]
28. Millersburg
29. Nelsonville (no primary)
30. Norwood
31. Oakwood (primary only)
32. Oberlin (colored—no primary)
33. Oberlin (white—no primary)
34. Orrville
35. Oxford
36. Paulding
37. Springfield
38. Shadyside
39. Shaker Heights
40. Upper Arlington (grades 1–6)
41. Van Wert
42. Vermilion
43. Warren
44. Washington Court House
45. Waynesfield
46. West Liberty (grades 1–6)
47. West Mansfield
48. West Union
49. Willard
50. Worthington (primary only)

A number of communities in Pierce County, North
Dakota, were also studied.

[1] Primary as used in this study means kindergarten and grades one, two, and
three.

How coöperation was secured. A letter was written to each of the school heads whose coöperation we wished to secure (see Appendix III). As will be noted in the letter, the purpose of the study was indicated and it was suggested that an assistant would probably call on the superintendent later.

The purpose of this visit to approximately one half of the centers was not only to secure the coöperation of these heads of schools, but also to convince them of the great importance of accuracy in securing the data.

CHAPTER IV

CHILDREN'S COMPANIONS AT THE MOVIES

THE effect of motion-picture experiences upon the child is partly dependent upon the circumstances surrounding attendance. Therefore, we cannot study thoroughly the effect of motion pictures upon the behavior of the child without considering the persons with whom he attends the motion-picture theater. It is possible that the good or bad effect of motion pictures is related in some degree to the child's companions.

The effect of companionship can be illustrated by noting what is likely to happen should the parents accompany the child to the motion-picture theater. The first part of the total activity of motion-picture attendance may likely arise in a home situation, perhaps in a discussion as to whether or not the evening is to be spent at a motion-picture theater. This may be followed by a conversation as to the nature of the motion pictures available that evening, assuming, of course, that one lives in a city where choice is possible. The parent may suggest that the child consult the rating of the pictures as found in *The Parents' Magazine* or *The Educational Screen*. If satisfactory newspaper and magazine reviews are available, these may also be consulted. Even if there happens to be only one motion-picture theater in the town, there is little doubt that the parents' point of view has in some way affected the decision as to whether or not a picture shall be viewed.

Now let us accompany the child and his parent to the motion-picture show. A young child may inquire about the meaning of certain things thrown on the screen. If the parent believes that there are certain aspects of the motion picture which might have a harmful effect upon the child, he may say to his child, for example, that "real life isn't like that," or "do you think you would have done the same thing as the man in the picture?" or "what did you think about what the little boy did?" In other words, he can point out to the child consequences or antecedents which the picture failed to supply or which it inadequately or inappropriately developed.

We are safe in assuming that when a child attends a motion picture with an older relative, there is an opportunity presented for lessening the more harmful effects of the motion picture. Indeed, the very prescription in a number of statutes that children under certain ages must be accompanied by their elders indicates that legislative bodies feel that the possible harm of such attendance may be thus diminished. Another benefit that is likely to be gained from parental companionship is supervision of the conduct of the child while at the motion-picture theater. The parents may also point out the significant values of the picture, not only in the content or story, but in acting, directing, and photography, and thus develop in the child the ability to appraise motion pictures.

Some of the effects of parental accompaniment have been suggested. Other companions may also change the nature of the total event of motion-picture attendance. Attendance alone may lead to some of the unfortunate consequences recounted by Dr. Thrasher in a companion volume. Or attendance alone might be beneficial through the opportunity it affords the child to reflect on what has occurred on the

screen. The relation of unaccompanied attendance to the
age and sex of the child may throw some light on the problem
of the socialization of boys and girls. Companionship with
brothers and sisters, with friends, with some one else, might
also furnish further clues to the study of the total effects of
motion-picture attendance on individuals.

Data from this study. The data relative to companions at
the movies were collected by question 9 on the inquiry
blank, which was phrased as follows:

9. The X's in the squares below tell when I went alone to the
"movies" in the last seven days and when I went with someone.

WITH WHOM I WENT	DAYS OF THE WEEK						
	Sun.	Mon.	Tues.	Wed.	Thur.	Fri.	Sat.
Father							
Mother							
Father and mother							
Brother or sister							
My own friends....							
Someone else							
By myself							

Table 1 presents the data secured on the companions of
the boys, and Chart 1 offers a picture of the change from
year to year in the percentage of attendances of boys with
various companions. At the eight-year age level 6.3 per
cent of the attendances of the boys are with their fathers.
The number decreases from this point and is negligible in

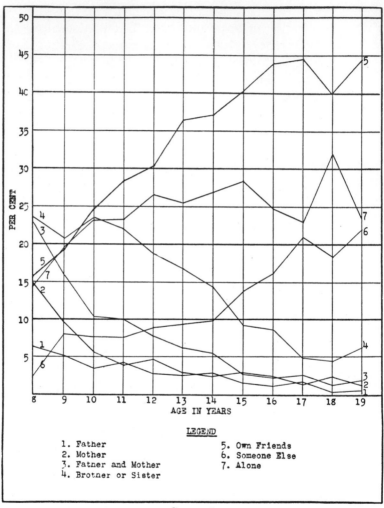

CHART 1
Comparison of boys' companions at the movies by ages

amount with the high-school boys. The mother as a companion of the boys ranks higher than the father, beginning at approximately 15 per cent, but decreasing very sharply in the first few years.

The line showing mothers and fathers together as companions of the boys starts at approximately 23 per cent, drops abruptly to 10 per cent at the ten-year age level, and then decreases gradually until, at the age of fifteen, 3 per cent or less of the attendances of boys are with their fathers and mothers as companions. In nearly every instance companionship of both the father and mother is equal to or more than that of the father, singly, and mother, singly, combined.

The line showing the percentage of boys who are accompanied by brothers or sisters begins at 24 per cent, drops to 21 per cent at the nine-year age level, rises again at the ten-year age level, and from this point on there is a constantly decreasing tendency for the boy to be accompanied by his brothers or sisters.

TABLE 1

BOYS' COMPANIONS AT THE MOVIES

Per cent of boys accompanied by each type of companion. Based on data from grades 4 to 12

Age	Father	Mother	Father and Mother	Brother or Sister	Their Own Friends	Some One Else	No Companion	No Data
8	6.30	14.96	22.83	23.62	15.75	2.36	14.17	0.01
9	5.09	9.50	15.83	20.73	19.10	7.87	19.19	2.69
10	3.96	5.56	10.23	23.36	24.49	7.64	23.34	1.42
11	4.15	3.87	10.02	22.02	28.33	7.58	23.19	0.83
12	2.72	4.61	7.69	18.62	30.30	8.78	26.57	0.70
13	2.51	2.93	6.06	16.65	36.34	9.19	25.50	0.82
14	2.87	2.43	5.39	14.28	37.20	9.88	26.91	1.03
15	1.45	2.85	2.81	9.17	40.28	13.73	28.35	1.36
16	1.11	2.38	2.33	8.63	43.99	16.20	24.56	0.79
17	1.66	1.39	2.63	4.92	44.55	20.86	22.94	1.03
18	0.32	2.21	1.27	4.43	40.02	18.35	31.80	1.58
19+	0.62	1.25	1.88	6.25	44.38	21.88	23.13	0.63
Total	2.63	3.65	6.37	14.81	34.77	11.48	25.18	1.10

Boys attend in increasing amounts with their own friends, starting at 16 per cent at the eight-year age level and reaching its highest point at the seventeen-year age level (45 per cent). There is a drop at the eighteen-year age level, followed by a rise at the nineteen-year age level. This latter change, however, may not be statistically significant.

The number who attended with some one else at the eight-year age level is about 2 per cent. There is an abrupt rise to 8 per cent at the nine-year age level, then the number changes hardly at all until the fourteen-year age level is reached. At this point the curve starts upward and reaches its highest point at nineteen years, 22 per cent.[1]

The line showing the percentage of boys who attend alone starts at 14 per cent, rises gradually to 28 per cent at the age of fifteen, fluctuates downward, rises again, and is highest, 32 per cent, at the eighteen-year age level.

At the eight-year age level 2 per cent of the girls' attendances are with their fathers (see Chart 2 and Table 2). The number increases slightly at nine, and then it decreases gradually and is negligible in amount at the high-school age. The mother as a companion of the girls begins at 33 per cent at eight, declines abruptly to about 15 per cent at nine, and then gradually tapers off, always remaining above the curve depicting the companionship of the father.

The line showing the mother and father together as companions of girls begins at 22 per cent and declines gradually to 2 per cent at the eighteen-year age level. There is a rise again at nineteen, but the number of cases at this point is exceedingly small. At the nine, ten, eleven, twelve, thirteen, and nineteen plus age levels, the father and mother

---

[1] Unfortunately the categories "some one else" and "my own friends" were not defined. The shape of the curves would lead one to believe that "dates," that is, the boy escort or his girl companion, were in some cases placed under "some one else."

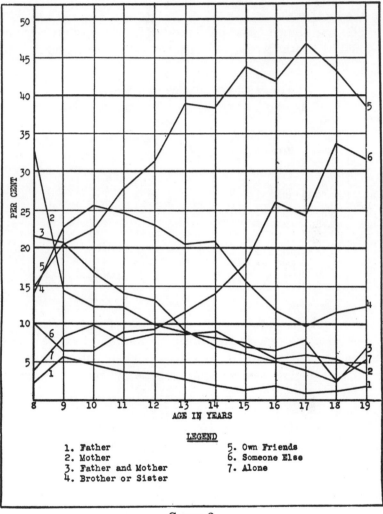

CHART 2

Comparison of girls' companions at the movies by ages

as companions exceeds accompaniment by either the father or the mother alone.

The line showing the percentage of girls who are accompanied by brothers or sisters begins at 14 per cent and rises to

TABLE 2

GIRLS' COMPANIONS AT THE MOVIES

Per cent of girls accompanied by each type of companion. Based on data from grades 4–12

Age	Father	Mother	Father and Mother	Brother or Sister	Their Own Friends	Some One Else	No Companion	No Data
8	2.16	33.09	21.58	13.67	14.39	10.07	3.60	1.44
9	5.64	14.54	20.57	22.74	20.47	6.43	8.23	1.39
10	4.66	12.31	16.82	25.61	22.48	6.42	9.94	1.76
11	3.67	12.20	14.08	24.76	27.81	9.02	7.70	0.76
12	3.52	9.87	13.17	23.16	31.31	9.30	8.72	0.92
13	2.66	8.51	8.77	20.46	39.04	11.48	8.46	0.63
14	1.86	8.21	7.02	20.81	38.36	13.94	9.03	0.77
15	1.18	7.39	6.11	15.66	43.87	18.02	6.94	0.84
16	1.83	5.25	4.95	11.85	41.96	26.20	6.35	1.59
17	0.79	5.95	3.89	9.75	46.95	24.26	7.77	0.63
18	1.02	5.55	2.29	11.48	43.37	33.67	2.30	0.51
19+	1.75	3.51	7.02	12.28	38.60	31.58	5.26	0.00
Total	2.63	9.13	9.83	18.99	35.77	14.77	7.89	0.98

26 per cent, its highest point, at the age of ten. It then declines to a plateau at the thirteen- and fourteen-year age levels, drops down to 10 per cent at the seventeen-year age level, and then rises only slightly for the two remaining ages.

The line depicting companionship with their own friends starts at 14 per cent and has an almost unbroken rise to 47 per cent at the seventeen-year age level. The line then drops to 43 per cent at the age of eighteen, and to 39 per cent at nineteen. This category exceeds every other one at almost every point. The percentages of attendances with brothers or sisters is similar to that of their own friends between the ages of ten and eleven. From then on, companionship with brothers or sisters gradually decreases while that with their own friends increases.

Girls who attend with some one else make up about 10 per cent of the attendances at the eight-year age level. There is a decline to 6 per cent at the nine- and ten-year age levels, a slight rise to 9 per cent at the eleven- and twelve-year age levels. From this point on, the curve rises sharply to 26 per cent at age sixteen, then experiences a slight downward movement at seventeen. It rises to 34 per cent at the eighteen-year age level, where it tapers off slightly.

Four per cent of the attendances of eight-year-old girls are alone. There is an abrupt rise to 8 per cent at the nine-year age level and from this point the line runs almost parallel to the base until the eighteen-year age level, at which point there is an abrupt drop.

COMPARISON OF BOYS' AND GIRLS' COMPANIONS

Charts 3 and 4 enable us to make comparisons of boys' and girls' companions at the movies by ages and per cents. Chart 3 compares the data for the companionship of father, mother, and father and mother. It will be noted that the line depicting the father as companion of both boys and girls is fairly close for all the age groups. For the mother as a companion, however, the two lines are widely separated at the lowest age level, but the difference gradually decreases as the child becomes older. The same comment applies to the lines depicting the father and mother as companions.

In practically every case we find that the boys are less frequently accompanied by their parents than are the girls. Chart 4 shows the comparison for brother or sister, own friends, some one else, and no companion. The lines of brother or sister, which are number 4 on the graph, have approximately the same shape for both boys and girls. Only at the age of eight years are the boys accompanied by brothers or sisters more frequently than are the girls. Lines

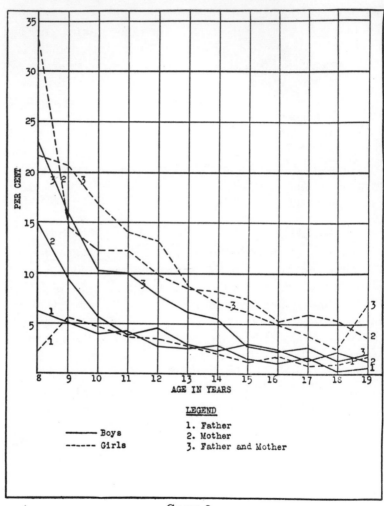

CHART 3
Comparison of boys' and girls' companions at the movies by ages

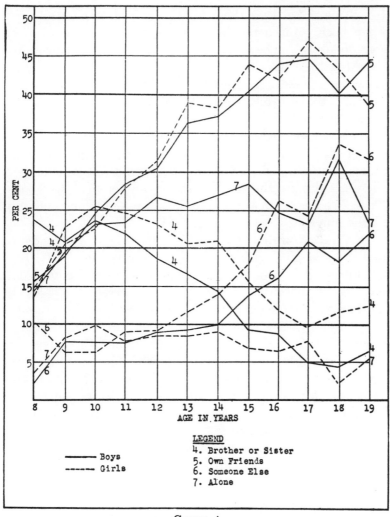

CHART 4

Comparison of boys' and girls' companions at the movies by ages

number 5 indicate the companionship of their own friends. It will be noted that these lines follow almost exactly the same path. Lines number 6 show the companionship of some one else. They have a tendency to remain fairly close together, but become of increasing width as the child grows older. Lines number 7, which show attendance alone, indicate the greatest disparity between the two groups. There is very little change in these lines for the girls except at the eighteen-year age level. With the boys, however, there is a steady increase in the percentage of the group who attend alone, up to the fifteen-year age level, from which point there is a drop to the sixteen- and seventeen-year age levels. There is a rise again at the eighteen-year age level and a drop at the nineteen-year age level.

In Chart 5 are compared the percentages of attendance of boys and girls with the various companions. The bars are arranged in order of increasing frequency for the companions of the girls. These figures represent averages for all the ages. These data are also presented in Tables 1 and 2. The most striking difference between the companions of boys and girls is in their attendances alone. Eight per cent of the girls' attendances are alone, while 25 per cent of the boys' attendances are alone. By far the most common type of companion is one's own friends. Thirty-five per cent of the boys go with their own friends and 36 per cent of the girls are so accompanied.

The following list shows the relative order of frequency of companions of boys and girls from lowest to highest:

Boys	*Girls*
Father	Father
Mother	No companion
Father and mother	Mother
Some one else	Father and mother

Boys	Girls
Brother or sister	Some one else
No companion	Brother or sister
Own friends	Own friends

CONCLUSIONS

What suggestions should be given to parents and others concerning desirable motion-picture companions for children? The data show a tendency for less and less parental accompaniment of children. Is this not a healthy sign, a sign of the growing maturity of the child in his ability to interpret properly what is shown on the screen? Would it not be undesirable to continue to make the child dependent upon the parents for interpretation of the picture that is shown?

Many persons are of the opinion that a significant proportion of children are unable to interpret properly the events which they see on the screen. Literally hundreds of times one notes there a portrayal of character and depiction of conduct which give totally erroneous notions of an event as it actually occurs in real life or as it might occur in an ideal situation. A mature adult who has a wide range of experiences can at once discount in some degree what he sees on the screen or can appreciate an ideal which is presented. Very frequently, however, the immature child or youth who has not been brought into contact with such experiences is in no way able to formulate a satisfactory judgment and can only acquiesce in what he sees there.

Surely we would not want to give up the principle of decreasing supervision of children as they become increasingly mature. There is probably no greater hindrance to character development than oversolicitude on the part of parents regarding the experiences and training which their

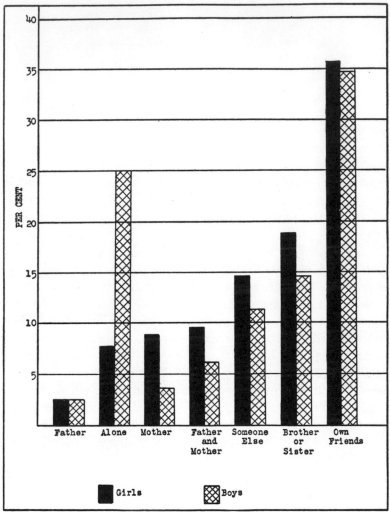

CHART 5
Comparison of boys' and girls' companions at the movies

children are receiving. The suggestion given here, however, is not that there be continuous parental accompaniment for all ages, but that every parent make certain that his child, if unsupervised, is able to interpret satisfactorily those experiences which he secures from the screen.

It is patent that when the time comes for an individual to break home ties, he should have had satisfactory training in being "on his own." Therefore, the function of the parent previous to this time is to train the child to accept the responsibilities and duties of self-directed action. It seems reasonable to conclude that the present situation has developed not from a strict adherence to this principle, but rather because parents have failed to recognize the need for training their children in motion-picture appreciation.

How can parents and others be trained to carry out their responsibilities in this regard? It would appear that they must first familiarize themselves thoroughly with what is shown on the screen. They ought to formulate in their own minds the characteristics of the motion pictures which are presented. When parents have achieved the ability to evaluate motion pictures two further steps are suggested. Parents might be encouraged to attend motion pictures *with* their children more frequently than they do now, and they might be urged to develop in their children this ability to evaluate what is shown on the screen. The education of both parents and children with respect to motion-picture evaluation should aid in securing more wholesome programs and should tend to decrease the possible harmful influences which attend the viewing of undesirable pictures.

CHAPTER V

FREQUENCY OF ATTENDANCE OF CHILDREN AT MOTION PICTURES

In Chapter I it was pointed out that 14.6 per cent of the audiences in the Columbus theaters was composed of children under the age of fourteen, and that 36.7 per cent were minors. The evidence points unmistakably toward the conclusion that large numbers of children are attending motion pictures every week. This type of evidence is inadequate, however, for an answer to the more critical question: To what extent is the motion-picture theater influencing every child? It may be possible, for example, that the high percentages of children found in motion-picture audiences are caused by excessive attendance on the part of a relatively few children.

The data here reported were secured on the questionnaires, Inquiry Blanks A and B (Appendix I), from 52,203 school children in Ohio.

It will be noted in Tables 3 and 4 that, at every age level, a larger percentage of boys than girls attended. It will be noted further that the pattern of attendance in the primary grades differs markedly from that shown by grades 4 to 12 (the youngest in the latter group was 8 years old, the oldest over 19). It is clear that by the time the fourth grade is reached, the pattern of weekly attendance at the motion picture is quite well established. Of the entire group of boys and girls in this sample, 53 per cent attended the movie at least once during the seven day period.

When one considers the primary grades as a group, 22 per

TABLE 3

MOTION-PICTURE ATTENDANCE OF BOYS FOR A SEVEN-DAY PERIOD

Age	Total number of pupils who attended	Total number attendances	Mean	Total number of pupils	Mean attendances for all pupils	Total number who did not go	Per cent not attending	Number never attending	Per cent never attending
I								
5–8	2,685	4,038	1.50	8,723	0.46	6,038	69.22	1,778	20.38
II								
8	84	119	1.42	134	0.89	50	37.31	10	7.46
9	661	984	1.49	1,056	0.93	395	37.41	89	8.43
10	970	1,568	1.62	1,476	1.06	506	34.28	118	7.99
11	1,093	1,674	1.53	1,627	1.03	534	32.82	96	5.90
12	1,340	2,134	1.59	1,878	1.14	538	28.65	97	5.17
13	1,440	2,303	1.60	1,997	1.15	557	27.89	69	3.46
14	1,382	2,134	1.54	1,927	1.11	545	28.28	64	3.32
15	1,382	2,191	1.59	1,926	1.14	544	28.25	58	3.01
16	1,113	1,886	1.69	1,598	1.18	485	30.35	28	1.75
17	870	1,388	1.60	1,193	1.16	323	27.07	20	1.68
18	373	654	1.75	502	1.30	129.	25.70	10	1.99
19+	107	175	1.64	163	1.07	56	34.36	2	1.22
9–19+a	1,294	2,231	1.72	2,124	1.05	830	39.08	112	5.27
8–19+	12,109	19,441	1.61	17,610	1.10	5,492	31.20	773	4.39
Total	14,794	23,479	1.59	26,324	0.89	11,530	43.80	2,551	9.69

a In this group differentiations were not made for each age.

TABLE 4

MOTION-PICTURE ATTENDANCE OF GIRLS FOR A SEVEN-DAY PERIOD

Age	Total number of pupils who attended	Total number attendances	Mean	Total number of pupils	Mean attendances for all pupils	Total number who did not go	Per cent not attending	Number never attending	Per cent never attending
I									
5–8......	2,131	2,970	1.39	8,027	0.37	5,896	73.45	1,899	23.66
II									
8........	93	130	1.40	166	0.78	73	43.98	11	6.63
9........	660	930	1.41	1,143	0.81	483	42.26	122	10.67
10.......	858	1,212	1.41	1,487	0.82	629	42.30	162	10.89
11.......	959	1,326	1.38	1,643	0.81	684	41.63	143	8.70
12.......	1,143	1,570	1.37	1,915	0.82	772	40.31	118	6.16
13.......	1,240	1,777	1.43	1,912	0.93	672	35.15	103	5.39
14.......	1,271	1,838	1.45	1,972	0.93	701	35.55	97	4.92
15.......	1,343	1,926	1.43	2,118	0.91	775	36.59	82	3.87
16.......	1,081	1,601	1.48	1,642	0.98	561	34.17	45	2.74
17.......	809	1,224	1.51	1,291	0.95	482	37.34	24	1.86
18.......	274	396	1.45	387	1.02	113	29.20	5	1.29
19+.....	40	54	1.35	76	0.71	36	47.37	6	7.89
9–19+ [a]..	1,068	1,730	1.62	2,100	0.82	1,032	49.14	122	5.81
8–19+....	10,839	15,714	1.45	17,852	0.88	7,013	39.28	1,040	5.83
Total....	12,970	18,684	1.44	25,879	0.72	12,909	49.88	2,939	11.36

[a] In this group differentiations were not made for each age.

cent report that they never attend. For both groups, the mean per cent who do not attend is 11. This average is heavily weighted, however, by the primary group. Complete abstinence from motion-picture attendance becomes very slight once we move outside the kindergarten and the first three grades.

It is interesting to see that the attendance of those who actually go in the primary group is almost the same as for the older group. That this represents a highly selected group is suggested by the fact that 71 per cent of the primary group did not attend in the seven-day period. The attendance of those who go in the seven-day period is never less than one. As before, the average attendance of the boys who go is greater than that of the girls.

We may estimate on the basis of these data that the average boy and girl in the primary grades attends slightly less than once every two weeks, or, more exactly, each child will average twenty-two attendances a year. However, almost 22 per cent of this group never attend the motion pictures, so the 78 per cent who do attend will, of course, average more than twenty-two attendances in a year.

When the attendance of the boys is compared with that of the girls, the picture changes somewhat. We can predict that the average girl in the primary grades will attend nineteen motion pictures a year and the average boy in this group will attend twenty-four motion pictures. Twenty per cent of the boys never attend and 24 per cent of the girls never attend. We see, therefore, that the influence of the motion picture extends even to our youngest school children.

The 35,453 boys and girls in grades 4 to 12 attended 35,155 times during the week studied. This means that the average attendance for this group is once a week. The number of pupils in this group who never attend, however, is only slightly more than 5 per cent of the group.

TABLE 5

MOTION-PICTURE ATTENDANCE OF BOYS AND GIRLS FOR A SEVEN-DAY PERIOD

Age	Total number of pupils who attended	Total number attendances	Mean	Total number of pupils	Mean attendances for all pupils	Total number who did not go	Per cent not attending	Number never attending	Per cent never attending
I									
5–8......	4,816	7,008	1.46	16,750	0.42	11,934	71.25	3,677	21.95
II									
8........	177	249	1.41	300	0.83	123	41.00	21	7.00
9........	1,321	1,914	1.45	2,199	0.87	878	39.93	211	9.60
10.......	1,828	2,780	1.52	2,963	0.94	1,135	38.31	280	9.45
11.......	2,052	3,000	1.46	3,271	0.92	1,218	37.35	239	7.31
12.......	2,483	3,704	1.49	3,793	0.98	1,310	34.54	215	5.67
13.......	2,680	4,080	1.52	3,905	1.04	1,229	31.44	172	4.40
14.......	2,653	3,972	1.50	3,899	1.02	1,246	31.96	161	4.13
15.......	2,725	4,117	1.51	4,044	1.02	1,319	32.62	140	3.46
16.......	2,194	3,487	1.59	3,240	1.08	1,046	32.28	73	2.25
17.......	1,679	2,612	1.56	2,484	1.05	805	32.41	44	1.77
18.......	647	1,050	1.62	889	1.18	242	27.22	15	1.69
19+.....	147	229	1.56	239	0.96	92	38.49	8	3.35
9–19+..[a]	2,362	3,961	1.68	4,224	0.94	1,862	44.08	234	5.54
8–19+.....	22,948	35,155	1.53	35,453	0.99	12,505	35.23	1,813	5.11
Total.....	27,764	42,163	1.52	52,203	0.81	24,439	46.82	5,490	10.52

[a] In this group differentiations were not made for each age.

TABLE 6

FREQUENCY OF GIRLS' ATTENDANCE DURING A SEVEN-DAY PERIOD

| Age in years | Number of times attended during seven-day period | | | | | | | | | | Total |
| | 0 | | 1 | | 2 | | 3 | | 4 or more | | |
	Number	Per cent	Number	Per cent	Number	Per cent	Number	Per cent	Number	Per cent	
8	64	42.38	61	40.40	18	11.92	6	3.97	2	1.32	151
9	342	39.40	376	43.32	106	12.21	26	2.99	18	2.08	868
10	434	39.13	471	42.47	150	13.53	36	3.25	18	1.62	1,109
11	481	39.88	518	42.95	150	12.44	38	3.15	19	1.58	1,206
12	538	37.34	634	44.00	208	14.43	51	3.54	10	0.70	1,441
13	489	33.20	670	45.48	237	16.09	54	3.67	23	1.57	1,473
14	546	35.85	645	42.35	253	16.61	58	3.81	21	1.38	1,523
15	588	36.39	677	41.89	258	15.97	70	4.33	23	1.42	1,616
16	392	32.08	531	43.45	209	17.10	78	6.38	12	0.98	1,222
17	259	27.55	420	44.68	194	20.63	47	5.00	20	2.13	940
18	89	27.99	145	45.60	63	19.81	19	5.97	2	0.63	318
19	29	45.31	26	40.63	7	10.94	2	3.13	—	—	64
Total	4,251	35.63	5,174	43.37	1,853	15.53	485	4.06	168	1.41	11,931

TABLE 7

FREQUENCY OF BOYS' ATTENDANCE DURING A SEVEN-DAY PERIOD

Age in years	Number of times attended during seven-day period											Total
	0		1		2		3		4 or more		
	Number	Per cent	Number	Per cent	Number	Per cent	Number	Per cent	Number	Per cent	
8.........	44	35.48	54	43.55	20	16.13	5	4.03	1	0.81	124
9.........	274	33.09	368	44.44	131	15.82	35	4.23	20	2.42	828
10.........	338	30.62	467	42.30	189	17.12	70	6.34	40	3.63	1,104
11.........	369	30.60	522	43.28	214	17.74	74	6.14	27	2.22	1,206
12.........	388	27.09	637	44.48	280	19.56	84	5.87	43	3.00	1,432
13.........	390	26.42	682	46.21	269	18.22	84	5.69	51	3.46	1,476
14.........	428	28.80	682	45.89	260	17.50	77	5.18	39	2.63	1,486
15.........	420	28.23	637	42.81	300	20.16	85	5.71	46	3.09	1,488
16.........	390	28.80	577	42.61	240	17.73	82	6.06	65	4.80	1,354
17.........	262	25.51	464	45.18	197	19.18	70	6.82	34	3.31	1,027
18.........	105	25.18	191	45.80	70	16.79	28	6.71	23	5.52	417
19.........	39	30.23	58	44.96	24	18.60	4	3.10	4	3.10	129
Total........	3,447	28.56	5,339	44.23	2,194	18.18	698	5.78	393	3.25	12,071

When the girls are considered separately from the boys, differences in average attendance are discovered similar to those found with the younger children. The mean attendance of the boys is 1.10 times per week and that of the girls is .88. Or, expressed in average attendances per year, the average girl goes forty-six times and the average boy fifty-seven times.

The data presented include the entire group of Ohio pupils studied and it becomes desirable to present information of a more detailed nature on the motion-picture habits of boys and girls. To secure this information a sampling of 11,931 records from the girls' group, ages eight through nineteen, was taken, and a sampling of 12,071 boys of the same age groups was used. Tables 6 and 7 present the material separately for the girls and boys relative to attendance not at all, once, twice, three times, and four or more times during the previous week.

The following table summarizes the data.

TABLE 8

SUMMARY OF FREQUENCY OF ATTENDANCE OF BOYS AND GIRLS AT MOTION PICTURES

Number of times	Boys	Girls
	Per cent	Per cent
0	29	36
1	44	43
2	18	16
3	6	4
4 or more	3	1

It is significant that 71 per cent of the boys went one or more times and 64 per cent of the girls so attended. The data are presented graphically by years in Chart 6.

A study of this chart reveals the following facts. The lines numbered 1 indicate the percentage of boys and girls who attended once during the seven days under study. It will be noted that there are approximately 44 per cent who

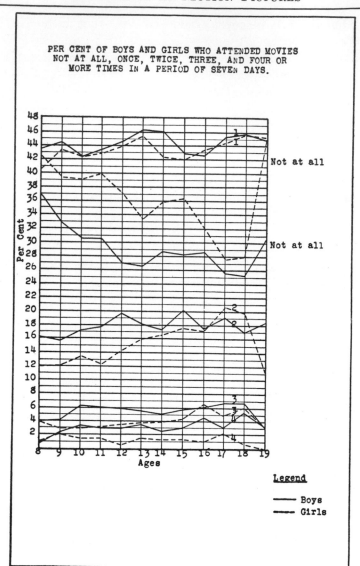

PER CENT OF BOYS AND GIRLS WHO ATTENDED MOVIES
NOT AT ALL, ONCE, TWICE, THREE, AND FOUR OR
MORE TIMES IN A PERIOD OF SEVEN DAYS.

CHART 6

so attended and that the variation with age is slight. Further, the percentage of boys and girls who attended once remains approximately the same for both groups.

The next two lines labeled "not at all" show considerable variation for boys and girls, however. Both drop to a low point at the age of thirteen, rise again, and drop to the lowest point at the seventeen-year age level where they come close to each other.

At the eight-year age level 12 per cent of the girls and 16 per cent of the boys attend twice a week. There is a slight movement upward to the seventeen-year age level where the highest point is reached. Both lines drop slightly at the eighteen-year age level. The curve for the boys rises here to the nineteen-year age level while that of the girls drops to a point lower than that of the eight-year-old girls.

The curve showing attendance three and four times a week change only slightly with ages. The boys attend with these frequencies more often than do the girls.

Chart 7 will enable the reader to get a graphic contrast between attendance of boys and girls and also to see more clearly the extent to which attendance at motion pictures has become a national weekly habit among children in cities or villages where motion pictures are accessible. Let us suppose that we have before us one hundred boys and one hundred girls who are typical of the group whom we studied. The extent of shading of the dots indicates the amount of attendance. Let us first ask of them this question: "How many of you went to the movies four times or more last week?" Three of the one hundred boys would raise their hands. This is shown by the three dots which are entirely black. Only one girl would answer this question affirmatively—this is shown by the single black dot. A further study of the chart will reveal the answers which one hundred typi-

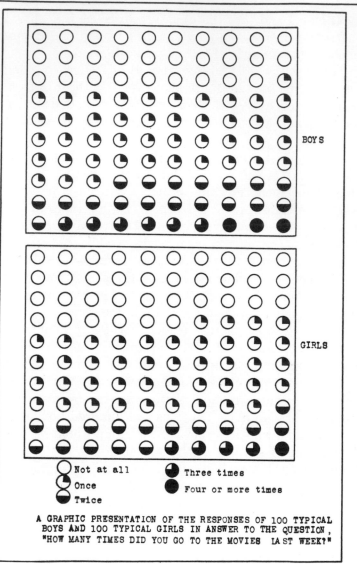

A GRAPHIC PRESENTATION OF THE RESPONSES OF 100 TYPICAL
BOYS AND 100 TYPICAL GIRLS IN ANSWER TO THE QUESTION,
"HOW MANY TIMES DID YOU GO TO THE MOVIES LAST WEEK?"

CHART 7

cal boys and girls would give in reply to questions relative to their attendance three times a week, twice, once, and not at all.

Usual Attendance

The question, "How often do you usually go to the movies?" was placed on the inquiry blank in order to provide a check on the question of the frequency of their attendance in the last seven days. A comparison of the percentages secured by the two different methods follows:

	Boys		Girls	
	Usual	Last 7 days	Usual	Last 7 days
Once a week	43.2	44	39.3	43
Twice	16.0	18	13.2	16
Three times	4.0	6	2.4	4
Four times or more	1.8	3	.7	1

We see here that there is a high degree of agreement between the two sets of figures, thus suggesting the validity of the data secured. We note also a tendency for a constant difference to appear between the two sets of data, with the usual attendance always slightly below that which was secured by getting a report on the last seven days of attendance. We have assumed in this study that the more accurate report was secured when the pupils indicated the frequency of their attendance for the seven-day period which had just passed.

	Per cent who did not go to movies in the seven-day period
Adena	33
Logan County	83
Belle Center	85
De Graff	70
Johnstown	55
Kinsman	81
Lakeview	71
Waynesfield	73
West Liberty	77
West Mansfield	78
West Union	55

TABLE 10

PREVIOUS INVESTIGATIONS OF MOTION-PICTURE ATTENDANCE

No.	Date	Investigator	City	Grades	Number	Sex	Average per week[c]	Range	Per cent not attending
1	1914	Foster, W. T.	San Francisco	3-8 Public School		B & G	—	—	10
2	1916	Cunningham, B.	Toledo			B & G	Slightly less than two	0-7	
3	1916	Johnson, George E.	Cleveland	1-8		B & G	1.5 m.		
				8-12		B	1.5 m.		
				8-12		G	1+m.		
4	1922 Spring	Perry, C. A.	Cities of the U. S.	9	17,310 boys in all	B	1.26 m.		
				9		G	1.04 m.		
				10		B	1.32 m.		
				10	20,195 girls in all	G	1.10 m.		
				11		B	1.24 m.		
				11		G	1.03 m.		
				12		B	1.06 m.		
				12		G	.99 m.		
				9-12		B	1.23 m.		
				9-12		G	1.05 m.		
5	1923	Berg, H. O.	Milwaukee	4-8	3,468	B & G	1.6 m.	1-6	
6	1923	Groves, J. W.	California	4	167	B & G	.76 m.		
				5	126	B & G	.93 m.		
				6	129	B & G	.77 m.		
				7	160	B & G	1.22 m.		
				8	172	B & G	1.19 m.		
				4-8	754	B & G	.98 m.		
7	1923	Hughes, Bertha	Evansville	8-18 (ages)	4,000	B & G	1.5	1-8	
8	1923	Jones, Irma S.	New York City, Ethical Culture School	3-8	343	B & G	.70		

TABLE 10—*Continued*

PREVIOUS INVESTIGATIONS OF MOTION-PICTURE ATTENDANCE—*Continued*

No.	Date	Investigator	City	Grades	Number	Sex	Average per week[c]	Range	Per cent not attending
9	1927	Trow, W. C.	Cincinnati	12	107	B & G	1.3 m.		
10	1928 Winter	Chase, Sara	Springfield, Mass.	4–6	102	B	.35 m.[a]		20.6
				4–6		G	.20 m.[a]		26.2
11		May-Jones	New York City	Elem.	615	B & G	1.7 m.		
12		Mitchell	Chicago	5–12	6,015	B	1.6 m.		
				5–12	4,037	G			
13	1929 Fall	Lewerenz, A.	Los Angeles	4–6	257	B & G	1.4 m.	0–6	
				4–6	324	B & G	1.6 m.	0–6	
14	1929 Fall	Theisen	Milwaukee	7–8	5,887	B & G	1.92 med.[b]	0–8	
				4–8	4,485	B & G	1.83 med.[b]	0–8	
				J.H.S.	2,602	B & G	1.83 med.[b]	0–8	
				9	217	B	2.03 med.[b]	0–10	
				10	195	B	2.24 med.[b]	0–6	
				11	132	B	2.01 med.[b]	0–8	
				12	105	B	1.80 med.[b]	0–5	
				9–12	649	B	2.05 med.[b]	0–10	
				9	219	G	2.06 med.[b]	0–6	
				10	203	G	1.86 med.[b]	0–5	
				11	141	G	1.92 med.[b]	0–5	
				13	115	G	1.96 med.[b]	0–5	
15	1929–30	Nelson, J. F.	New York City	9–12	678	B	1.98 med.[b]	0–6	
16	1929–30	Shuttleworth	Group of cities	4–5–6	692	B & G	1.4 m.	0–7	
				7–8–9	4,843	B & G	1.1 m.	0–5	
17	1931	Lewerenz, A.	Los Angeles	11-year-olds	254	B & G	1.2 m.		
18	Spring	Seagoe	Los Angeles	1–8	800	B & G	.95		39

a Based on Saturday and Sunday only. Statements of "one or two" attendances per week tabulated as two.

b These represent a maximum.

c Means are indicated by the letter "m," medians, by "med." In some instances the report did not indicate whether the average given was a mean or median. These figures are followed by no code.

That children in the small Ohio villages which include in their school population children from the outlying farms attend motion pictures less frequently than do children in the larger cities is indicated by preceding data on villages under 250 in population.

Further evidence of the fact that children in rural schools attend less frequently than children in city schools where motion-picture theaters are accessible is contained in the data from 1,050 children in Pierce County, North Dakota. We see in Table 9, for example, that in these villages, none of which is over 250 in population, children attend motion pictures rarely.   That the cause is almost wholly one of physical inaccessibility is shown by the fact that the mean attendance in the county seat, Rugby, is .71.

TABLE 9

ATTENDANCE DATA FOR RURAL OR VILLAGE SCHOOLS IN PIERCE COUNTY, NORTH DAKOTA

School	Boys			Girls			Both		
	Number	Attendances	Mean	Number	Attendances	Mean	Number	Attendances	Mean
Tunbridge.	33	1	.03	42	8	.19	75	9	.12
Wolford...	60	6	.10	75	4	.05	135	10	.08
Orrin......	52	15	.29	65	11	.20	117	26	.22
Selz........	28	6	.21	30	5	.17	58	11	.14
Miscellaneous......	101	19	.19	113	29	.26	214	48	.22
Total.....	274	47	.17	325	57	.14	599	104	.7

OTHER STUDIES

All the major studies in the field of motion-picture attendance have been reviewed and their major findings reported in Table 10. It cannot be pointed out too strongly that every study which has been made in this field corroborates the findings presented in this chapter.   In general, the mean weekly attendances are higher than those secured by the writer. This is probably due to the fact that the earlier studies were not made during a period of financial depression as was this one.

CHAPTER VI

TIME OF ATTENDANCE OF CHILDREN AT MOTION PICTURES AND DURATION OF STAY

INFORMATION concerning the time of day when children attend motion pictures, the day when they attend, and the length of stay, is basic to a thoroughgoing study of the social effects of such attendance. For example, the further development of Saturday and Wednesday matinée programs for children will depend in large measure for its success upon the degree to which it can utilize current motion-picture habits of children. If children now attend frequently in the afternoon, the development of such matinées offers fewer difficulties than would matinées which conflict significantly with children's habits of attendance.

MOST FREQUENT DAYS OF ATTENDANCE

In Table 11 we have indicated the percentage of attendance by boys and girls for the seven days of the week. A study of this table shows the following facts:

The attendance of boys as an entire group varies only slightly from that of girls with the exception of Wednesday when the attendance of girls is greater than that of boys. Saturday is the day of most frequent attendance. Nearly one third of all the boys and girls who were studied attended on this day. This fact is an important one for motion-picture policy-making. If a satisfactory *Saturday* motion-picture program can be provided for boys and girls then one third of the children will benefit from it.

45

Sunday is the day next in importance for motion-picture attendance. Slightly more than one fourth of all the motion-picture attendances of boys and girls occur on Sunday.

The Saturday and Sunday attendances combined account for more than one half of the children who go. If a satisfactory *Saturday and Sunday* motion-picture program can be provided for boys and girls then more than one half of the children will benefit from it. These figures must be modified, of course, in those cities or states which prohibit Sunday movies.

Friday follows Saturday and Sunday in the percentage of attendance of boys and girls. Approximately one eighth of all the attendances occur on Friday. It should be noted that about one third of all attendances are on Saturday, one fourth on Sunday, and one eighth on Friday. Thursday, with approximately 6 per cent of the attendances, is the lowest day of the week, followed closely by Tuesday and then by Monday. The order of attendance by days from highest to lowest is: Saturday, Sunday, Friday, Wednesday, Monday, Tuesday, Thursday.

TABLE 11

PER CENT OF BOYS AND GIRLS IN ATTENDANCE AT MOTION PICTURES
ON EACH DAY OF THE WEEK

Day	Boys	Girls	Boys and girls
Sunday......................	27.37	26.12	26.81
Monday......................	7.13	7.18	7.15
Tuesday......................	6.00	6.23	6.11
Wednesday...................	7.96	9.30	8.55
Thursday.....................	5.72	6.17	5.92
Friday......,................	11.74	11.28	11.55
Saturday.....................	34.06	33.71	33.91

When we add up the Friday, Saturday, and Sunday attendances, we find that 72 per cent or approximately three fourths of all the attendances are concentrated on week-end days and nights.

If a satisfactory *week-end* motion-picture program can be provided for boys and girls then almost three fourths of the children will benefit from it.

There is, however, a difficulty encountered in this concentration of attendance on the week-end. Evidence presented in Table 20 indicates that adults also concentrate their attendance on the week-end. As a result, we find a clash of interests at such motion pictures, since the motion-picture exhibitor is anxious to capitalize on this huge influx of customers, adults and children.

It has not been demonstrated, of course, that a real conflict *always* exists between the interests of adults and children. There is no reason why some motion-picture programs might not appeal to and benefit both adults and children.

No attempt is made here to present a plan by means of which the problem may be entirely solved.

The high attendances over the week-end are facts. The development of programs for Friday, Saturday, and Sunday which will be of benefit to children, will be the largest single contribution to a solution of the motion-picture problem.

Most Frequent Hour of Attendance

There are some who believe that attendance at evening motion pictures may interfere with the health of the children. Data are presented in a companion study which give evidence on this point. By linking such data with the facts here presented one may ascertain more satisfactorily the extent to which evening attendance may be affecting the health of children.

Further, evening motion-picture attendance of children offers problems of supervision. There is no implication here that·the evening hours should not be used for such attendance. But it is a fact that evening attendance demands greater self-reliance on the part of children and youth.

Finally, evening attendance, especially on school nights, may interfere with school work. We present no evidence to show that motion-picture attendance does so interfere. We do make available data which show the extent to which children attend motion pictures during various days of the week in order that harmful influences, if found, can be checked against attendance habits.

Tables 12 and 13 present a comparison of the attendance of boys and girls according to time of day.

TABLE 12

ATTENDANCE OF BOYS AT EACH AGE LEVEL ACCORDING TO TIME OF DAY

Age	Morning		Afternoon		Evening		Total Number
	Number	Per Cent	Number	Per Cent	Number	Per Cent	
8.......	3	2.52	57	47.90	59	49.58	119
9.......	28	2.85	432	43.90	524	53.25	984
10.......	55	3.51	648	41.33	865	55.17	1,568
11.......	56	3.35	638	38.11	980	58.54	1,674
12.......	65	3.05	764	35.80	1,305	61.15	2,134
13.......	65	2.82	758	32.91	1,480	64.26	2,303
14.......	57	2.67	572	26.80	1,505	70.52	2,134
15.......	67	3.06	491	22.41	1,633	74.53	2,191
16.......	40	2.12	395	20.94	1,451	76.94	1,886
17.......	33	2.38	263	18.95	1,092	78.67	1,388
18.......	20	3.06	90	13.76	544	83.18	654
19.......	4	2.29	22	12.57	149	85.14	175
Total....	493	2.86	5,130	29.81	11,587	67.33	17,210

It is evident from these tables that morning motion-picture programs would run counter to the present general motion-picture habits of children. The assumption is not made here that this habit would be difficult to change.

TABLE 13

ATTENDANCE OF GIRLS AT EACH AGE LEVEL ACCORDING TO TIME OF DAY

Age	Morning		Afternoon		Evening		Total Number
	Number	Per Cent	Number	Per Cent	Number	Per Cent	
8.......	5	3.85	48	36.92	77	59.23	130
9.......	29	3.12	360	38.71	541	58.17	930
10.......	29	2.39	505	41.67	678	55.94	1,212
11.......	34	2.56	567	42.76	725	54.68	1,326
12.......	42	2.68	664	42.29	864	55.03	1,570
13.......	57	3.21	667	37.54	1,053	59.26	1,777
14.......	58	3.16	560	30.47	1,220	66.38	1,838
15.......	31	1.61	539	27.99	1,356	70.40	1,926
16.......	21	1.31	376	23.49	1,204	75.20	1,601
17.......	20	1.63	230	18.79	974	79.58	1,224
18.......	9	2.27	68	17.17	319	80.56	396
19.......	1	1.85	8	14.81	45	83.33	54
Total....	336	2.40	4,592	32.84	9,056	64.76	13,984

Attention is called to the fact that the motion-picture habits of children are already fixed in another area, and that the success of morning programs will be dependent in some measure upon the degree to which this habit can be modified.

It is also evident that there is a promising field for the development of afternoon programs for younger children. Such afternoon programs would have the merit that they would not interfere as markedly with adult viewing of motion-picture programs as would evening programs.

It should be remembered, however, that the evening, not the afternoon, is "dating" time. Further, evening motion-picture attendance, especially when it is in the downtown theaters, is accompanied by far more thrill than is the afternoon attendance. Evening motion-picture attendance is more of an adventure than attendance in the afternoon. The evening is the time when grown-ups go. It is the socially approved time for going. Further, the afternoon offers opportunity for recreational activities which depend upon daylight and cannot be carried on in the evening. This would tend to cause motion-picture attendance to be deferred until the evening in order that the other recreational activities may be carried on in the afternoon.

PROGRAM OFFERINGS MOST FREQUENTLY VIEWED

Table 14 presents data concerning the percentage of boys and girls in grades 4 to 12 who watched the main picture, newsreel, and comedy once, twice, and three or more times. These data are therefore indications of the time spent in the theater. It seems reasonable, also, to use them to interpret the popularity of each of these program features.

TABLE 14

PERCENTAGE OF BOYS AND GIRLS WHO WATCHED THE MAIN PICTURE, NEWSREEL, AND COMEDY ONE, TWO, AND THREE OR MORE TIMES

	Main picture		Newsreel		Comedy	
	Boys	Girls	Boys	Girls	Boys	Girls
Only once..........	80	82	79	85	72	79
Twice..............	19	17	20	14	26	20
Three or more times..	1	1	1	1	2	1

These data have also been expressed as average number of viewings for each age and are shown graphically in Chart 8. The lines showing the average number of viewings of the comedy show that there is always a constant difference between the boys and the girls, the latter spending less time re-viewing the comedy at every age level. The curve for the boys begins at 1.5, rises slightly, and then is almost continuously downward until the seventeen-year age level, when it smoothes off. The curve for the comedy has approximately the same shape for the girls although the line moves

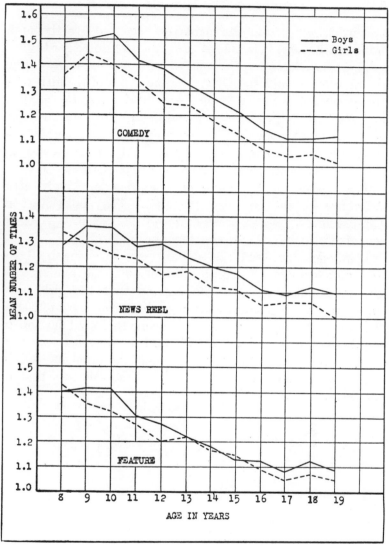

CHART 8

Mean number of times the comedy, newsreel, and feature were viewed by boys and girls

51

upward rapidly from the eight-year age level to the nine, from which point it is almost continuously downward.

The curve depicting the number of times the boys viewed the newsreel is consistently higher than that of the girls with the exception of the eight-year age level where the number of cases is not large. The lines begin at 1.3 with the boys and girls and rise for the boys at the nine-year age level, but no such rise is experienced for the girls. At the nineteen-year age level the boys' mean is 1.1 while that of the girls is 1.0.

The curves for the main picture show strikingly little difference for the boys and the girls. They both start at approximately 1.4 and finish at about 1.1. From thirteen to seventeen they are approximately the same.

Differences between the amount of re-viewing by boys and girls cannot be accepted as prima facie evidence of greater popularity unless we assume that the girls were under no greater restrictions regarding time spent at the theaters than were the boys. Bearing this qualification in mind, we may say that the girls and boys were equally interested in the main picture, but that the girls' interest in the newsreel and the comedy was not so great as that of the boys.

CHAPTER VII

THE AGE COMPOSITION OF THE MOTION-PICTURE AUDIENCE

THIS chapter will describe the techniques used and the results secured in studying the composition of motion-picture audiences. The data for this study were secured by Mrs. Charles Carr under the direction of Professor Mary Louise Mark of the Department of Sociology, Ohio State University.

It would be highly desirable to have accurate evidence as to the number of children and adults of every age who attended motion-picture theaters. Since the conditions under which the data were gathered precluded this possibility, it was necessary to use four different age groupings. Two factors entered into the selection of these groups, namely, (1) the selection of groups of ages which could be distinguished, and (2) the utility of the data to be secured.

The first group consisted of children less than seven years of age, and it was not tallied by sex because of the difficulty of accurate judgment. This phase of the study was made in the spring of 1929, just prior to the advent of sound motion pictures, and it was assumed that this first group would be the non-readers and would in general, except in the upper limit, include children not in school. The second group, ages seven to thirteen, inclusive, was selected because it is a normal age range of children in the second to the eighth grades. Within these age limits will lie the bulk of elementary school pupils. The third

53

group, ages fourteen to twenty, composes what one roughly thinks of as the ages of youth or adolescence. The fourth group, the adults twenty-one years of age and over, constituted a clear-cut and natural grouping of mature individuals.

Since these ages were only estimated by the observers, the age groups were made sufficiently large to admit of fairly accurate estimation. The graduate students who were responsible for checking most of the theaters had had teaching experience in the elementary school and were therefore acquainted with younger children. The reliability (consistency) of the method is attested by the fact that when this technique was later used in a motion-picture attendance study in New York City, it was discovered that there was high agreement among observers relative to the age groups in which children should be placed. It is assumed that errors in estimation are compensating, and that there is no bias in either direction that will not be corrected through the use of several different judges.

It was decided to conduct the study at Columbus, Ohio, first, because it is a typical American city, and second, because of administrative advantages. Through the Motion Picture Theater Owners' Association of Ohio, important data were gathered concerning the theaters to be studied, namely, the names, addresses, and seating capacities of all the theaters in the city that were members. This included the majority of privately owned houses. Similar data were easily obtained from the larger chain-owned houses. By checking this list with the telephone directory and with the city directory, it was possible to locate all the theaters operating at the time the study began. When this list of theaters was later compared with the theaters listed in the county for taxation, it was found to be complete.

The next step was to visit the owners or managers of the theaters to obtain permission to station students at their houses to analyze the attendance for a week if it seemed desirable to do so. The following information was also obtained:

a. Seating capacity of the theater.

b. Whether or not Negroes were admitted and if so whether the number admitted at any one time was limited. Two theaters, for instance, reserved half the seats for Negroes and refused to sell more tickets to them when their half was filled, while another small theater reserved only the last two rows in the rear for colored patrons.

c. The hours the ticket office was open each day in the week. This information was necessary in order that provisions could be made for a worker to cover the theater at every possible time that patrons enter.

d. The prices of admission for adults and children to all places in the theater and at all times during the day. Some theaters have matinée prices while others charge the same at all times. Some charge less for balcony seats than for main-floor seats, but others have one price for all seats.

This information was gathered on a three-by-five card in this form:

Name of Theater	Address
Name of Owner	Address
Hours Open during Week:	Prices:
Sunday	Children
Week Days	Adults
Capacity	Negroes

·This information was the basis for choice of the fifteen theaters to be studied out of the total of forty-three that were open when the study was made. Table 15 shows the seating capacities of the Columbus motion-picture theaters. The fifteen theaters were chosen to yield the greatest variety of size, location, type of clientele, and class of offerings. In making this selection, the first step was to spot the theaters on a map of the city in order to show definitely their

TABLE 15

SEATING CAPACITIES OF COLUMBUS THEATERS

Theater	Capacity	Theater	Capacity
Linden [a]	764	Avondale	500
Majestic	1,000	Champion	500
New	475	Clinton	1,000
Northern	550	Columbia	450
Park	300	Capital	360
Piccadilly	500	Dixie	475
Pythian [b]	700	Dreamland	780
Rialto	350	Dunbar [b]	350
Ritz	700	Eastern	1,500
Rivoli	650	Empress	600
Royal	298	Exhibit	400
Savoia	415	Fifth Avenue	275
Southland	493	Franklin	210
State	1,600	Garden	700
Thurmania [b]	525	Grand	1,200
Cameo	560	Hippodrome	310
Victor	1,000	Hollywood [b]	603
Victoria	290	Innis	800
Wilmar	250	Knickerbocker	900
Wonder	350	Lamar's Hudson	600
Ogden	900	Lamar's Parsons	600
Loew's Broad	2,800	Lincoln	350
Alhambra	490	Loew's Ohio	3,300
		Keith Albee-Palace	3,013

Total capacity—35,736   Total capacity of theaters studied—10,947

[a] Those in italics are the ones selected for study.
[b] Closed either temporarily or permanently.

distribution; anyone familiar with the sections of the city could then easily choose theaters representative of the different types of neighborhoods. Prices proved a very good index to the class of features shown at the various theaters. On the basis of the price of admission and of the general judgment as to the theater's clientele obtained from the managers or owners, it was evident that all houses in the city could be classified under headings as follows:

a. Good downtown theaters showing up-to-date films in modern houses with a patronage of the better type. The prices were 35 cents and 50 cents during evening hours.

b. Poor downtown theaters, showing old or inferior pictures, patronized largely by men. The prices were 10 cents and 20 cents at all times.

c. Good all-Negro theaters, modern, showing same run of pictures as in better class of white theaters. The prices were higher than the poor neighborhood houses, indicating a better type of patronage and newer shows.

d. Good neighborhood theaters, in better residential districts, showing modern pictures of desirable type, in attractive houses. The usual admission charge for adults was 30 cents.

e. Poor neighborhood theaters, situated in poorer neighborhoods, usually on the edge of business districts, showing cheap pictures in old houses, frequently admitting Negroes to part of the house. The price of this group was never over 20 cents and was usually about 10 or 15 cents.

The forty-three theaters were divided into the five groups described and samples of the houses in each class were taken for study, their location kept in mind. The selection therefore includes houses in all parts of the city and covers one all-Negro theater, two good downtown houses, six in good neighborhoods, two poor downtown, and four poor neighborhood theaters. Table 16 shows the Columbus theaters and the ones which were selected for study.

TABLE 16

SIZE GROUPINGS OF COLUMBUS THEATERS, AND THEATERS WHICH WERE
SELECTED FOR STUDY [a]

Seating Capacity			
Up to 400	401–700	701–1,000	1,001–3,300
Lincoln [a]	*Champion*	*Majestic*	*Eastern*
Exhibit	*Northern*	*Knickerbocker*	*Grand*
Park	*New*	Clinton	State
Rialto	*Savoia*	*Linden*	Loew's Broad
Royal	*Empress*	*Innis*	Keith-Albee
Victoria	*Southland*	Ogden	Palace
Wilmar	*Piccadilly*	Dreamland	Loew's Ohio
Capital	Ritz	Victor	
Fifth Avenue	Rivoli		
Franklin	Cameo		
Hippodrome	Alhambra		
Wonder	Avondale		
	Columbia		
	Dixie		
	Garden		
	Lamar's Hudson		
	Lamar's Parsons		

[a] Those in italics are the ones selected for study.

Are the fifteen theaters which we used representative
of the entire forty-three theaters open in Columbus? The
following data give the answer to this question.

Group	Number of theaters	Number sampled
Up to 401	12	2
401–700	17	6
701–1,000	8	5
1,000–3,300	6	2
Total	43	15

It will be noted that we sampled one sixth of the theaters up to 400 seating capacity, approximately one third of
those in the group from 401 to 700, five eighths of those from
701 to 1,000, and one third of those from 1,001 to 3,300.

Or, when we consider them in two size groupings, we took exactly one half of the theaters over 701 in seating capacity, and eight twenty-ninths of those under 700 in seating capacity.

It will be noted that we took two fifths of the good downtown theaters, one half of the poor downtown theaters, one all-Negro theater, approximately one fifth of the poor neighborhood houses, and approximately two fifths of the good neighborhood houses.

The study was made in March, April, and May 1929. It was spread out over this period of time in order to increase the accuracy of the data. The estimates, as indicated above, were made by a few people who, *through practice and careful supervision*, had learned to estimate ages with high reliability. Second, it seemed desirable also to have all kinds of weather conditions represented in order that exceedingly good or bad weather might be equally well represented in its good or bad effects upon attendance. In the same fashion, the extension of time over three months made it possible for the effects of exceedingly popular or unpopular pictures to be equally distributed.

Table 17, Column 1, presents the number and percentage of persons found in the audiences of the fifteen Columbus theaters which were studied. No weighting is here used. Column 2 presents the data secured when the average data for each size of theater were appropriately weighted by the number of theaters in that group. Four different size groupings were used, *and in the group containing the largest downtown theaters separate calculations were made for each of the downtown theaters not included in the study. This was done in order that their varying capacities might be taken into account.* Column 3 indicates the data secured when the theaters were divided into five types, good downtown, poor downtown, all-Negro, good neighborhood, and poor neighborhood. The large downtown theaters were separately considered as in the previous instance. Although there are significant statistical differences in certain instances, nevertheless there are no socially significant differences that are readily apparent.

TABLE 17

WEIGHTED AND UNWEIGHTED DATA ON THE AGE COMPOSITION OF COLUMBUS MOTION-PICTURE AUDIENCES

Age groups	1 Unweighted		2 Weighted by size		3 Weighted by type	
	Number	Per cent	Number	Per cent	Number	Per cent
Under 7......	2,056	3.1	5,764	2.5	6,808	2.8
7–13........	9,155	13.7	25,267	10.8	28,246	11.8
14–20........	13,928	20.8	50,827	21.7	53,023	22.1
21 or more....	41,795	62.4	152,673	65.1	151,650	63.3
Total........	66,934	100.0	234,531	100.0	239,727	100.0

We have assumed in this study that the weighted data in Column 3 present the most accurate picture of motion-picture attendance in the Columbus theaters, since one need make fewer assumptions in accepting these data as valid than when the unweighted data or the data weighted according to size are used. It will be noted, further, that in three of the four cases the means for the group weighted by type of theater lie in between the means of the other two groupings.

May we repeat the critical data found in Table 17?

In the Columbus theaters in a typical week there were 239,727 estimated attendances. Of this group 6,808 attendances (2.8 per cent) were by children under seven years of age. There were 28,246 attendances by boys and girls (11.8

per cent) seven to thirteen years of age. Of those who attended 53,023 (22.1 per cent) were children from fourteen to twenty years of age, and 151,650 were adults twenty-one years of age or over. Minors constituted 36.7 per cent of the audience and adults 63.3 per cent. On the basis of these data we must conclude that whatever effects motion pictures are having, good or bad, these effects are being widely distributed in our population.

Table 18 presents the data from the theaters themselves. When we compare the theaters by groups we see important differences in the percentage of children under seven years of age who are attending each type of theater. We see clearly that it is in the neighborhood house where we can expect to find the highest percentage of children under seven years of age. The smallest number of children under seven years was found in a good downtown theater, number 1, which had only 0.7 per cent children under seven years. The highest percentage of young children found in any theater was discovered in a poor neighborhood house, number 15, which had 12.9 per cent of children under seven years of age.

In the group seven to thirteen years of age, the smallest percentage of children, 3.0 per cent, was found in theater number 2, a good downtown theater, and the largest, 38.1 per cent, at theater number 12, a poor neighborhood theater. We note also that the good neighborhood theaters had the highest total percentage of children from seven to thirteen years of age.

Column 3 in Table 18 summarizes the data from Columns 1 and 2, and presents the percentage of children in the theater who are thirteen years of age or under. The small poor downtown theater, number 4, had the smallest percentage of children in this group, 4.5 per cent; and theater number 12, a poor neighborhood theater, had the highest,

TABLE 18

AGE DISTRIBUTION OF AUDIENCES, IN THE WEEK UNDER OBSERVATION
BY THEATER AND BY TYPE

Theater	Per Cent					
	1	2	3	4	5	6
	Under 7 (1)	7 to 13 (2)	13 or under (1+2)	14 to 20 (3)	Under 21 (1+2+3)	21 or more (4)
Good downtown						
1.	0.7	4.8	5.5	28.5	34.0	66.0
2.	2.5	3.0	5.5	18.2	23.7	76.3
Mean....	1.4	4.1	5.5	24.5	30.0	70.0
Poor downtown						
3.	1.6	7.4	9.0	15.2	24.2	75.8
4.	0.5	4.0	4.5	6.5	11.0	89.0
Mean....	1.3	6.7	8.0	13.2	21.2	78.8
All-Negro						
5.	2.0	12.7	14.7	21.3	36.0	64.0
Good neighborhood						
6.	4.6	19.2	23.8	19.0	42.8	57.2
7.	4.9	20.0	24.9	18.5	43.4	56.6
8.	2.0	30.0	32.0	21.4	53.4	46.6
9.	5.6	27.7	33.3	23.2	56.5	43.5
10.	6.1	20.9	27.0	17.4	44.4	55.6
11.	5.2	24.9	30.1	24.9	55.0	45.0
Mean....	4.7	23.2	27.9	20.3	48.2	51.8
Poor neighborhood						
12.	3.6	38.1	41.7	25.4	67.1	32.9
13.	5.9	20.2	26.1	23.2	49.3	50.7
14.	3.0	12.6	15.6	23.6	39.2	60.8
15.	12.9	16.6	29.5	18.0	47.5	52.5
Mean....	4.8	18.5	23.3	23.1	46.4	53.6
Total...............	3.1	13.7	16.8	20.8	37.6	62.4

41.7 per cent. The good neighborhood houses as a group, however, had the highest percentage of children thirteen years of age or under, followed closely by the poor neighborhood, by the all-Negro theater, by the poor downtown theater, and finally by the good downtown theater.

In the age group from fourteen to twenty, the smallest percentage of children, 6.5 per cent, was found at a small poor downtown theater, number 4; the largest, 28.5 per cent, at a good downtown theater, number 1. Interestingly enough, the highest mean percentage of children fourteen to twenty years of age was in the good downtown theater, where 24.5 per cent was found, followed closely by the poor neighborhood theater, and in turn by the good neighborhood theater, the all-Negro, and finally the poor downtown theater, which had only 13.2 per cent of children from fourteen to twenty years of age. When we add these three columns together to secure the percentage of minors, we discover that a poor downtown theater, number 4, a small one, had the smallest percentage of children, 11 per cent, while a poor neighborhood theater, number 12, had the highest, 67.1 per cent. The average percentages of minors for the various groups run in order from highest to lowest as follows:

Good neighborhood	48.2
Poor neighborhood	46.4
All-Negro	36.0
Good downtown	30.0
Poor downtown	21.2

Proportion of Males and Females in the Columbus Audiences

The proportion of males and females in the Columbus audiences was studied. No evidence is presented on the group under seven years of age because of the difficulty of accurate judgment. Table 19 presents the findings.

The fact that the total audience studied contained almost 10 per cent more males than females indicates that here is a factor that apparently has not been considered in the development of motion-picture programs. Indeed, the emphasis on romance and sentiment in motion pictures has been defended, in part at least, on the grounds that the preponderance of women in the audiences justified such themes.

TABLE 19

PERCENTAGE OF MALES AND FEMALES IN FIFTEEN COLUMBUS THEATERS

Theater	Age Groups					
	7–13		14–20		21 or More	
	Male	Female	Male	Female	Male	Female
Good downtown						
1.	57.5	42.5	57.2	42.8	54.3	45.7
2.	50.0	50.0	37.1	62.9	59.1	40.9
Poor downtown						
3.	62.7	37.3	68.9	31.1	75.2	24.8
4.	70.0	30.0	85.5	14.5	88.8	11.2
All-Negro						
5.	64.1	35.9	55.0	45.0	55.6	44.4
Good neighborhood						
6.	61.2	38.8	56.0	44.0	50.0	50.0
7.	69.2	30.8	54.2	45.8	48.9	51.1
8.	67.7	32.3	53.0	47.0	50.6	49.4
9.	62.3	37.7	57.2	42.8	55.8	44.2
10.	58.7	41.3	55.1	44.9	52.7	47.3
11.	53.9	46.1	54.9	45.1	53.9	46.1
Poor neighborhood						
12.	76.8	23.2	68.3	31.7	56.0	44.0
13.	66.2	33.8	60.5	39.5	57.0	43.0
14.	71.7	28.3	65.5	34.5	64.3	35.7
15.	69.8	30.2	63.3	36.7	63.4	36.6
Total...............	64.4	35.6	57.2	42.8	59.3	40.7

MOST FREQUENT DAYS OF ATTENDANCE AS DETERMINED BY ENUMERATION AT THE THEATER

Table 20 presents data on the age composition of the audience in reference to days of the week. In Chapter VI where we secured data directly from pupils by a questionnaire, we discovered that 72 per cent of the attendance of the reporting children was concentrated on Friday, Saturday and Sunday. If now, from Table 21 we take the similar data, we find that for the three age groups—under seven, seven to thirteen, and fourteen to twenty—67.1 per cent, 75.2 per cent, and 60.0 per cent, respectively, of the attendance was concentrated on these three week-end days.

TABLE 20

PERCENTAGE DISTRIBUTION OF PATRONS OF EACH AGE GROUP BY DAY
OF THE WEEK

Age	Percentage Distribution of Attendance						
	Sun.	Mon.	Tues.	Wed.	Thurs.	Fri.	Sat.
Under 7 years.	32.5	7.6	8.7	7.6	9.1	12.4	22.2
7–13.........	36.5	7.1	5.4	5.3	6.9	12.9	25.8
14–20........	27.3	8.7	10.8	10.1	10.4	13.5	19.2
21 or more....	24.8	11.0	10.6	11.0	11.0	13.7	17.8
Total.........	27.1	9.9	9.9	10.0	10.3	13.5	19.3

COMPARISON WITH HOLMES' FINDINGS

The data on the age composition of Columbus audiences
differ strikingly from those presented in the study by Dr.
Joseph L. Holmes of Columbia University.[1]   He discovered
that a median of 5.2 per cent of the total audience of 155,349
persons which he studied was under seventeen years of age.
We found at Columbus that 14.6 per cent of an estimated
total audience of 239,727 was composed of children *under
the age of fourteen*.   In other words, in our study of the age
composition of the Columbus motion-picture audience we
discovered almost three times as many children *under the age
of fourteen* as Dr. Holmes found in New York City *under the
age of seventeen*.   Further, in *The Motion Picture*,[2] the following statement was presented as a quotation of Dr. Holmes:

> On the average, minors constitute only 5.2 per cent of the
> total attendance.   That is, out of every 150,000 spectators, only
> 7,800 were likely to be under twenty-one years of age.

It will be noted that the age is given as twenty-one instead
of seventeen.

[1] "Crime and the Press," *Journal of Criminal Law and Criminology*, Vol. XX,
Nos. 1 and 2, May and August 1929.
[2] Vol. 5, no. 6, p. 3.   *The Motion Picture* is the house organ of the Motion Picture
Producers and Distributors of America.   Mr. Will H. Hays is president of the organization.

Since the findings of Dr. Holmes' study have been widely used to depreciate the importance of children as a significant part of the total movie audience, some space will be taken here to point out its crucial inadequacies.

1. No data are presented by Dr. Holmes to show the representativeness of the New York theaters sampled. As a matter of fact, there is good reason to believe that they are not only unrepresentative of the country at large, but that they do not even adequately represent the theaters in New York City. The data given in Table 21 are rough estimates by the writer of the total weekly attendance at each of the twelve theaters which Dr. Holmes studied. When we recall that the neighborhood houses which we studied had total weekly audiences of about 5,000, we realize that to designate any except perhaps theaters 2, 6, and 12 as *neighborhood* theaters is to use a descriptive term that is certainly meaningless outside of New York City.

TABLE 21

TOTAL WEEKLY AUDIENCE AT THE TWELVE NEW YORK CITY THEATERS COVERED IN THE HOLMES STUDY

Theater	Size	Theater	Size
1.	26,551	7.	12,747
2.	8,596	8.	17,787
3.	26,768	9.	37,870
4.	84,007	10.	53,361
5.	45,507	11.	35,112
6.	7,581	12.	6,601

2. No data are presented to show the validity of the use of Monday, Wednesday, and Saturday as a representative sampling of a week's attendance. In Chapter VI it was noted that 72 per cent of a total group of 52,241 Ohio school children attended motion pictures on Friday, Saturday, and Sunday. If this same condition obtains in New York

City, a sampling of only Monday, Wednesday, and Saturday may very likely give lower proportions of children in attendance than would be found in a complete week's study.

3. There seems to be no valid reason for eliminating one of the twelve theaters from consideration when estimating the percentage of children found in the audiences. One is at a loss, therefore, to account for Dr. Holmes statement that

> It would not be accurate to include the counts at the last theater in determining the average, for at this theater, one in a suburban town, pictures were exhibited but three days a week.[3]

To exclude from the final accounting the theater which had the highest percentages of children in its audience, namely, 26.5 per cent on Monday, 41.5 per cent on Wednesday, and 21.0 per cent on Saturday, is not defensible on the grounds stated.

4. Dr. Holmes reported his findings in terms of medians. As all the data here reported are in terms of means his data were reworked on that basis. The mean per cent of attendance under seventeen years of age for the eleven theaters was 6.0, for the entire group, 6.5.

5. When this study was made, New York State had a law which prohibited children under sixteen years of age attending a motion picture unless accompanied by an adult. Generalizations about the composition of the motion-picture audience are therefore inapplicable when they will include other states or cities which do not have such a regulation.

[3] *Ibid.*, p. 89.

CHAPTER VIII

THE NATIONAL AUDIENCE

To what extent can data relative to Columbus be considered typical of cities, towns, villages, or rural districts elsewhere? Are we justified in assuming that one would find as high proportions of children in motion-picture audiences in New York City, Rugby, North Dakota, or Jackson, Mississippi? We have already pointed out the high degree of similarity in children's motion-picture habits from city to city. The proportion of adults in a community is another important factor to be considered. It is important, therefore, to make such comparisons between Columbus and other communities.

When we compare Columbus with Ohio (1930 census) and then with the United States as a whole, we secure the following results:

Per cent of Population under Fifteen

Columbus	23.1
Ohio	27.4
United States	29.4

Per cent of Population under Twenty-Five

Columbus	40.2
Ohio	44.6
United States	47.7

We discover, therefore, that Columbus has 6.3 per cent fewer children under fifteen years of age than is true of the United States in general, and has 4.3 per cent less children than does the state of Ohio. Further, Columbus has

68

7.5 per cent fewer persons under twenty-five than is typical of the United States, and 4.4 per cent less than Ohio in general.

Additional data presented in Table 22 indicate the position of Columbus in relation to all the cities of Ohio having a population of 25,000 or over. Data for smaller cities are not available. The 1930 census data are used.

TABLE 22

PER CENT OF OHIO POPULATION UNDER FIFTEEN AND UNDER TWENTY-FIVE YEARS OF AGE IN CITIES HAVING MORE THAN 25,000 POPULATION (1930 CENSUS)

City	Per cent of population under fifteen years of age	Per cent of population under twenty-five years of age
1. Youngstown.........	30.7	48.6
2. Lorain.............	30.1	49.3
3. Warren............	29.0	46.6
4. Portsmouth........	28.8	47.5
5. Akron.............	28.7	46.8
6. Hamilton..........	28.3	46.5
7. Marion............	28.2	45.1
8. Steubenville.......	27.9	46.5
9. Canton...........	27.5	44.6
10. Cleveland.........	26.4	45.1
11. Lima..............	26.2	43.3
12. Zanesville.........	25.6	43.0
13. Springfield........	25.4	43.0
14. Newark...........	24.7	41.0
15. Toledo............	24.5	42.0
16. Dayton...........	24.2	42.1
17. Mansfield.........	23.9	41.2
18. COLUMBUS.......	23.1	40.2
19. Lakewood.........	23.0	38.6
20. Cincinnati........	22.1	39.3
21. East Cleveland.....	19.0	36.3

It will be noted from this table that Columbus ranks eighteenth in this group of twenty-one cities in its per cent of children under fifteen years of age, and ranks eighteenth in its per cent of population under twenty-five years of age. It would appear, therefore, that in considering the data that we secure from Columbus as an adequate sampling of other cities in the state, one is likely to err only on the side of securing a smaller proportion of children in the audience than would be true had other Ohio cities been used. It appears likely that were the study extended to cities having larger percentages of children the data would tend to show even larger percentages of children in the motion-picture audiences.

When Columbus is compared with the ten largest cities in the United States (1930 census), the data in Table 23 are secured. Here again it is interesting to note that Columbus ranks ninth in percentage of population under fifteen in this group of eleven cities, and ranks ninth in percentage of population under twenty-five. Only Los Angeles and St. Louis have smaller percentages of population under fifteen and under twenty-five years of age.

TABLE 23

RELATIONSHIP OF COLUMBUS TO LARGE AMERICAN CITIES IN REFERENCE TO PER CENT OF POPULATION UNDER FIFTEEN, AND UNDER TWENTY-FIVE YEARS OF AGE
(1930 CENSUS)

City	Per cent of population under fifteen years of of age	Per cent of population under twenty-five years of age
1. Detroit............	27.3	44.8
2. Pittsburgh.........	27.0	45.9
3. Cleveland..........	26.4	45.1
4. Baltimore..........	25.6	43.4
5. Philadelphia.......	24.9	42.9
6. Boston............	24.8	42.3
7. New York..........	24.4	42.9
8. Chicago...........	24.1	42.4
9. COLUMBUS........	23.1	40.2
10. St. Louis..........	21.8	39.8
11. Los Angeles........	19.6	35.3

It appears logical, therefore, to conclude that studies of the composition of motion-picture audiences in these larger American cities would show as high a proportion of children and minors as Columbus. Indeed, had the investigators been desirous of securing facts to support the conclusion that motion-picture audiences are composed of a high percentage of children, Columbus would hardly have been a wise choice. The fact that Columbus was chosen as the city to be studied in spite of the abnormally low percentage of children and minors is proof of the highly conservative nature of the findings.

Knowing the proportions of the various age groups attending theaters in Columbus, Ohio, how can we make use of the data to obtain similar information for the entire United States? Before this estimate can be attempted, it is necessary to have accurate figures for the total national weekly attendances at motion-picture theaters. When we have the total attendance and we have the percentage for each age group, it is a matter of simple arithmetic to calculate the numbers in each age group attending motion-picture theaters every week.

The organization known as the Motion Picture Producers and Distributors of America is responsible for the statement that in 1929 the average weekly audience at the motion-picture theaters numbered 115,000,000 attendances. Let us for the moment accept these figures as accurate. If 36.7 per cent of this weekly audience consisted of minors, then in 1929 the weekly attendance by minors was 42,205,000. Further, if 14.6 per cent were under fourteen years of age, then at least 16,790,000 persons of this group attended motion pictures every week.

There is good reason to believe that this estimated weekly attendance of 115,000,000 is incorrect. The 1930 census shows a population in the United States of 122,775,046 persons. Of this number 11,444,390 are under five years of age and would figure almost not at all as motion-picture habitués. We may estimate that there are 5,000,000 who are prevented, either through physical infirmity, incarceration in jails and penitentiaries, or other reasons, from attending commercial motion pictures. This leaves about 105,000,000 persons who are physically able to attend. If we divide the 115,000,000 attendances by this group of 105,000,000 people, we secure an average weekly attendance of slightly more than 1. That the true average attendance is not so high as this figure is suggested by the following facts.

The population of Franklin County, Ohio, was 361,055 in 1930. If we subtract from this number the estimated 13 per cent who are physically unable to attend, we have left about 315,000 persons. There were 239,727 estimated attendances for the week studied. This gives us an average of about three fourths of an attendance for each person physically able to attend. This figure is likely to be high if considered as an average for the country, because the area which made possible the 240,000 attendances was probably not Franklin County, but a much wider one. Columbus is a capital city and a university city as well, factors which produce a high number of transients—excellent movie patrons.

If we apply this index of .75 to the 150,000,000 possible attendants in the United States, we discover the weekly attendance to be 78,750,000 persons. This is probably a maximum since the weekly average for Columbus and for the country as a whole is probably lower than .75.

Another method of estimating national attendance shows also that the estimate of 115,000,000 weekly patrons is too high. It was discovered in the Columbus study that the index of weekly attendance in relation to seating capacity was approximately 7, that is, each seat was occupied seven times in the course of a week. The Motion Picture Producers and Distributors of America give figures showing that there are 11,000,000 seats in motion-picture houses in the United States. If this is accurate, the total weekly attendance in 1929 can be estimated to be 7 × 11,000,000, or 77,000,000.

If 36.7 per cent of this total audience of 77,000,000 weekly attendance is composed of minors, then we can expect that 28,259,000 minors were actually attending weekly in 1929. If 14.6 per cent of the total audience is under the age of fourteen, then among these 28,259,000 minors there will be 11,242,000 children under the age of fourteen.

According to the 1930 census, 31.3 per cent of the population is found to be between the ages of five and twenty inclusive. Since the group under four years of age contributes a negligible number to the motion-picture audience, we discover that 31.3 per cent of the children and youth contribute slightly less than 37 per cent of the members of our national motion-picture audience. Therefore, we can conclude that the percentage of children and youth in representative motion-picture audiences will be slightly greater than their percentage in the population of the country.

Conclusion

Data have been presented in this report to show that children and youth the country over are regular patrons of motion-picture theaters. Further evidence has been presented to show that they contribute a proportion of the total audience that is far greater than we have commonly been led to believe. The effect of motion pictures, therefore, is universal and this fact must be faced in a statesmanlike manner by exhibitors and producers, by teachers, and by parents.

APPENDIX I, INQUIRY BLANK A

January 10, 1930
Form A, Project 169

> Read
> Carefully
> BEFORE
> You
> Answer

Bureau of Educational Research
The Ohio State University

MOTION PICTURE ATTENDANCE

Edgar Dale, Investigator

1. My name is_____

2. I am a   BOY   GIRL

3. I am_____years old.

4. I am in Grade _____ in _____
                                                    (School)
   at _____
              (Town)   (State)

5. How often do you usually go to the "movies"?_____

6. If you go about every week, how many times a week do you usually go? _____

7. The last time I went to the "movies" I watched the main picture _____ times, the news reel _____ times, and the comedy _____ times. (If there was no news reel or comedy, leave that space blank. If there were two main pictures, count them as one.)

8. The X's in the squares below tell when I went to the "movies" in the last seven days.

Time of Day	Days of the Week						
	Sun.	Mon.	Tues.	Wed.	Thurs.	Fri.	Sat.
Forenoon..........							
Afternoon.........							
Evening...........							

9. The X's in the squares below tell when I went alone to the "movies" in the last seven days and when I went with someone.

With Whom I Went	Days of the Week						
	Sun.	Mon.	Tues.	Wed.	Thurs.	Fri.	Sat.
Father...............							
Mother..............							
Father and Mother.....							
Brother or Sister.......							
My own friends........							
Someone else..........							
By myself...........							

10. I have written this on _____
                      (Month)   (Day)   (Year)

ATTENDANCE OF PRIMARY CHILDREN

Grade...

Name of School...Name of

BOYS
TABLE I
FREQUENCY OF ATTENDANCE DURING THE LAST SEVEN DAYS

Number who did not go at all   ; number who went once   ;

twice   ; three times   ; four times   ; five times   ;

six times   ; seven times   ; eight times   Number

who say they never go to the "movies"

TABLE III
NUMBER OF BOYS WHO WENT TO THE "MOVIES"

Items	Number who went on							Totals
	S	M	T	W	Th	F	Sat	
Number in school today								
No. who went yesterday Morning								
Afternoon								
Evening								

TABLE V
WITH WHOM THEY WENT

Companions	Number who went on							Totals
	S	M	T	W	Th	F	Sat	
Father								
Mother								
Father and mother								
Brother or sister								
Their own friends								
Someone else								
By themselves								

Project 169
Form 1-a

AT COMMERCIAL MOTION PICTURES

Week ending..., 1930

Town and State...

GIRLS
TABLE II
FREQUENCY OF ATTENDANCE DURING THE LAST SEVEN DAYS

Number who did not go at all   ; number who went once   ;

twice   ; three times   ; four times   ; five times   ;

six times   ; seven times   ; sight times   Number

who say they never go to the "movies"

TABLE IV
NUMBER OF GIRLS WHO WENT TO THE "MOVIES"

Items	Number who went on							Totals
	S	M	T	W	Th	F	Sat	
Number in school today								
No. who went yesterday Morning								
Afternoon								
Evening								

TABLE VI
WITH WHOM THEY WENT

Companions	Number who went on							Totals
	S	M	T	W	Th	F	Sat	
Father								
Mother								
Father and mother								
Brother or sister								
Their own friends								
Someone else								
By themselves								

February 14, 1930
Form 1-b, Project 169

BUREAU OF EDUCATIONAL RESEARCH

THE OHIO STATE UNIVERSITY
COLUMBUS, OHIO

ATTENDANCE AT COMMERCIAL MOTION PICTURES OF CHILDREN ENROLLED IN KINDERGARTEN AND GRADES I, II, AND III

TO THE TEACHER: The data asked for in the six tables on the other side of this sheet relate to attendance at *commercial* motion pictures only—*not* to "movies" seen at home, club, church or school. These data should be supplied as follows:

Do not start to record the information on Monday. Greater accuracy of results will be secured by starting on some other school day.

Ask the pupils to keep a written record of every "movie" that they see each day for seven days, noting the time of day they go (morning, afternoon, or night) and the persons with whom they go. Such a record would look something like this: "Johnny Jones, Tuesday afternoon, mother; Friday night, father and mother." Collect these written records each morning. You will need them in order to give the information asked for in all six tables.

TABLE I: At the end of the seven-day period, refer to the five written records of attendance which each boy has handed you and record the number of boys who did not go at all, those who went once, twice, and so on, during the past seven days (ending yesterday). Also indicate the number who say they *never* go to the "movies."

TABLE II: On the basis of the girls' written records of their attendance, follow the same procedure as you did for the boys in Table I.

TABLE III: Each morning, after you have collected the boys' written records, please write in Table III the number who went yesterday morning, yesterday afternoon (before six o'clock), and yesterday evening (after six o'clock). Their attendance for Friday, Saturday, and Sunday—three days—must be on the written record they hand you on Monday morning.

TABLE IV: Enter the girls' attendance in the same manner as that of the boys in Table III.

TABLE V: Each morning, after you have recorded the information asked for in Tables III and IV, record the number of boys who, on their written records, say they went each day with their fathers, with their mothers, with their fathers *and* mothers, with their brothers *or* sisters, etc.

TABLE VI: Enter similar information for the girls as was recorded for the boys in Table V.

When your entries are completed and checked for accuracy, kindly send this sheet to your superintendent.

EDGAR DALE,
Investigator.

78

APPENDIX II

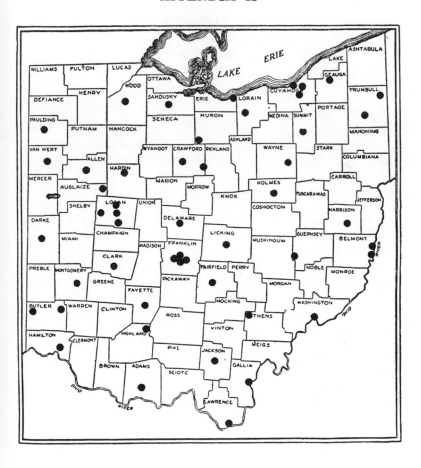

APPENDIX III

THE OHIO STATE UNIVERSITY
GEORGE W. RIGHTMIRE, *President*

COLUMBUS

COLLEGE OF EDUCATION
BUREAU OF EDUCATIONAL RESEARCH

January 14, 1930

DEAR SUPERINTENDENT:

Many organizations interested in child welfare wish to know how often children of various ages attend motion picture theaters, when they go, and with whom they go. This Bureau has agreed to coöperate with these agencies, since it believes that the collection of this information is a worth-while project. A grant from the Payne Fund, a local Ohio foundation, has made this research possible.

We are asking a few public school officials throughout the state to assist us, through their teachers, in gathering the data indicated on the enclosed form. These questions can be answered by the children in approximately fifteen minutes.

I am writing you, therefore, with the hope that you will allow us to collect from your pupils the information needed in this study. To make the collection easy for you we shall be glad to send our Mr. LaPoe to see you personally to arrange the details.

Since Mr. LaPoe will be in to see you within the next month, it will not be absolutely necessary for you to answer this communication, but I shall appreciate a reply.

Very cordially yours,
W. W. CHARTERS

INDEX

Age composition of motion-picture audience, 53-62

Attendance, motion-picture: afternoon, 4; children's companions, 4; communities studied, 12-13; comparison of Columbus, Ohio, audiences with New York, 65-67; evening, 4; findings of study, 1-3; methods used, 1-3; morning, 4-5; national audience, 68-69; popular days, 3, 45-47, 64-65; problem in character education of children, 6-10; proportion of males and females in Columbus audiences, 63-64; techniques used in investigation of children's habits, 11-14; time, 45-52; usefulness of data, 8-9; validity of data, 11-12

Audience, motion-picture: age composition of, 53-62; audience, national, 68-69

Carr, Mrs. Charles, 53

Character education, motion picture as problem in, 6-10

Children, attendance at motion pictures: companions, 4; communities studied, 12-13; effect of companionship, 15-29; frequency, 30-42; frequent days, 45-47; frequent hours, 47-50; morning, 4-5; problem, 6-10; program offerings most frequently viewed, 50-52; techniques used in determining, 11-14; time, 45-52; validity of data, 11-12

Columbus, Ohio, audiences attending motion pictures, compared with New York, 65-67

Comedy, popularity of, 50-51

Days, frequency of attendance at motion pictures, 64-65

Film Daily, quoted, 9

Hays, Will H., 65; quoted, 8
Holmes, Joseph L., 65-67; quoted, 67

Lasky, Jesse L., quoted, 8

Mark, Mary Louise, 53

Motion pictures, character education, 6-10; comparison of attendance, Columbus, Ohio, audiences compared with New York, 65-67; frequency of attendance by days, 64-65; national audience attending, 68-69; proportion of males and females in Columbus audiences, 63-64

Newsreel, popularity of, 51-52

Program offerings most frequently viewed by children, 50-52

Sampling, of children, 8, 12-13; of theaters, 56-60

Techniques, of securing attendance data, 1-3; of making study, 5-10; of securing age data, 53-57

Time of day, 1-4; most frequent, 46-52; spent at motion picture, 3

Usefulness of attendance data, 8

Validity of techniques, 11-12

THE EMOTIONAL RESPONSES OF CHILDREN
TO THE MOTION PICTURE SITUATION

MOTION PICTURES AND YOUTH

THE PAYNE FUND STUDIES

W. W. CHARTERS, CHAIRMAN

MOTION PICTURES AND YOUTH: A SUMMARY, by W. W. Charters, Director, Bureau of Educational Research, Ohio State University.

Combined with

GETTING IDEAS FROM THE MOVIES, by P. W. Holaday, Indianapolis Public Schools, and George D. Stoddard, Director, Iowa Child Welfare Research Station.

MOTION PICTURES AND THE SOCIAL ATTITUDES OF CHILDREN, by Ruth C. Peterson and L. L. Thurstone, Department of Psychology, University of Chicago.

Combined with

THE SOCIAL CONDUCT AND ATTITUDES OF MOVIE FANS, by Frank K. Shuttleworth and Mark A. May, Institute of Human Relations, Yale University.

THE EMOTIONAL RESPONSES OF CHILDREN TO THE MOTION PICTURE SITUATION, by W. S. Dysinger and Christian A. Ruckmick, Department of Psychology, State University of Iowa.

Combined with

MOTION PICTURES AND STANDARDS OF MORALITY, by Charles C. Peters, Professor of Education, Pennsylvania State College.

CHILDREN'S SLEEP, by Samuel Renshaw, Vernon L. Miller, and Dorothy Marquis, Department of Psychology, Ohio State University.

MOVIES AND CONDUCT, by Herbert Blumer, Department of Sociology, University of Chicago.

THE CONTENT OF MOTION PICTURES, by Edgar Dale, Research Associate, Bureau of Educational Research, Ohio State University.

Combined with

CHILDREN'S ATTENDANCE AT MOTION PICTURES, by Edgar Dale.

MOVIES, DELINQUENCY, AND CRIME, by Herbert Blumer and Philip M. Hauser, Department of Sociology, University of Chicago.

BOYS, MOVIES, AND CITY STREETS, by Paul G. Cressey and Frederick M. Thrasher, New York University.

HOW TO APPRECIATE MOTION PICTURES, by Edgar Dale, Research Associate, Bureau of Educational Research, Ohio State University.

THE EMOTIONAL RESPONSES OF CHILDREN TO THE MOTION PICTURE SITUATION

❖

WENDELL S. DYSINGER

DEPARTMENT OF PSYCHOLOGY,
STATE UNIVERSITY OF IOWA

CHRISTIAN A. RUCKMICK

PROFESSOR OF PSYCHOLOGY,
STATE UNIVERSITY OF IOWA

NEW YORK
THE MACMILLAN COMPANY
1933

THIS SERIES OF TWELVE STUDIES OF THE
INFLUENCE OF MOTION PICTURES UPON
CHILDREN AND YOUTH HAS BEEN MADE BY
THE COMMITTEE ON EDUCATIONAL RE-
SEARCH OF THE PAYNE FUND AT THE RE-
QUEST OF THE NATIONAL COMMITTEE FOR
THE STUDY OF SOCIAL VALUES IN MOTION
PICTURES, NOW THE MOTION PICTURE RE-
SEARCH COUNCIL, 366 MADISON AVENUE,
NEW YORK CITY. THE STUDIES WERE DE-
SIGNED TO SECURE AUTHORITATIVE AND
IMPERSONAL DATA WHICH WOULD MAKE
POSSIBLE A MORE COMPLETE EVALUATION
OF MOTION PICTURES AND THEIR SOCIAL
POTENTIALITIES

CHAIRMAN'S PREFACE

MOTION PICTURES are not understood by the present generation of adults. They are new; they make an enormous appeal to children; and they present ideas and situations which parents may not like. Consequently when parents think of the welfare of their children who are exposed to these compelling situations, they wonder about the effect of the pictures upon the ideals and behavior of the children. Do the pictures really influence children in any direction? Are their conduct, ideals, and attitudes affected by the movies? Are the scenes which are objectionable to adults understood by children, or at least by very young children? Do children eventually become sophisticated and grow superior to pictures? Are the emotions of children harmfully excited? In short, just what effect do motion pictures have upon children of different ages?

Each individual has his answer to these questions. He knows of this or that incident in his own experience, and upon these he bases his conclusions. Consequently opinions differ widely. No one in this country up to the present time has known in any general and impersonal manner just what effect motion pictures have upon children. Meanwhile children clamor to attend the movies as often as they are allowed to go. Moving pictures make a profound appeal to children of all ages. In such a situation it is obvious that a comprehensive study of the influence of motion pictures upon children and youth is appropriate.

To measure these influences the investigators who cooperated to make this series of studies analyzed the problem to discover the most significant questions involved. They set up individual studies to ascertain the answer to the questions and to provide a composite answer to the central question of the nature and extent of these influences. In using this technique the answers must inevitably be sketches without all the details filled in; but when the details are added the picture will not be changed in any essential manner. Parents, educators, and physicians will have little difficulty in fitting concrete details of their own into the outlines which these studies supply.

Specifically, the studies were designed to form a series to answer the following questions: What sorts of scenes do the children of America see when they attend the theaters? How do the mores depicted in these scenes compare with those of the community? How often do children attend? How much of what they see do they remember? What effect does what they witness have upon their ideals and attitudes? Upon their sleep and health? Upon their emotions? Do motion pictures directly or indirectly affect the conduct of children? Are they related to delinquency and crime, and, finally, how can we teach children to discriminate between movies that are artistically and morally good and bad?

The history of the investigations is brief. In 1928 William H. Short, Executive Director of the Motion Picture Research Council, invited a group of university psychologists, sociologists, and educators to meet with the members of the Council to confer about the possibility of discovering just what effect motion pictures have upon children, a subject, as has been indicated, upon which many conflicting opinions and few substantial facts were in existence. The university men proposed a program of study. When Mr. Short appealed to The Payne Fund for a grant to support such an investigation, he found the foundation receptive because of its well-known interest in motion pictures as one of the major influences in the lives of modern youth. When the appropriation had been made the investigators organized themselves into a Committee on Educational Research of The Payne Fund with the following membership: L. L. Thurstone, Frank N. Freeman, R. E. Park, Herbert Blumer, Philip M. Hauser of the University of Chicago; George D. Stoddard, Christian A. Ruckmick, P. W. Holaday, and Wendell Dysinger of the University of Iowa; Mark A. May and Frank K. Shuttleworth of Yale University; Frederick M. Thrasher and Paul G. Cressey of New York University; Charles C. Peters of Pennsylvania State College; Ben D. Wood of Columbia University; and Samuel Renshaw, Edgar Dale, and W. W. Charters of Ohio State University. The investigations have extended through four years, 1929–1932 inclusive.

The committee's work is an illustration of an interesting technique for studying any social problem. The distinctive characteristic of this technique is to analyze a complex social problem into a series of subordinate problems, to select competent investigators to work upon each of the subordinate projects and to integrate the findings of all the investigators as a solution of the initial problem. Such a program yields a skeleton framework, which, while somewhat lacking in detail, is substantially correct if the contributing investigations have been validly conducted. To provide this framework or outline is the task of research. To fill in the detail and to provide the interpretations are the natural and easy tasks of those who use the data.

W. W. C.

Ohio State University
June, 1933

AUTHORS' PREFACE

THIS investigation owed its origin to a plan of research laid out under the auspices of the Payne Fund. In the main it fitted into the general plan of the Committee on Educational Research of that organization and profited through the fertile questions recurrently raised by Mr. W. H. Short, director of the Motion Picture Research Council. At the same time the study represents a unit in a program of research carried on over a term of years in the Psychological Laboratory at the University of Iowa in the field of the emotions. The more significant of these studies are Bayley's A Study of Fear by Means of the Psychogalvanic Technique (*Psychol. Monog.*, 38, 1928, No. 4, 1–38); Patterson's A Qualitative and Quantitative Study of the Emotion of Surprise (*Psychol. Monog.*, 40, 1930, No. 1, 85–108); Dysinger's A Comparative Study of the Affective Responses by Means of the Impressive and Expressive Methods (*Psychol. Monog.*, 41, 1932, No. 4, 14–31); and Smith's Variations in the Galvanic Response (*Ibid.*, 142–152).

We wish here to acknowledge our indebtedness to the trustees of the Payne Fund for their continued financial support of this undertaking and to Dr. Charters and Mr. Short for their timely and renewed encouragement and valuable recommendations. It was also a source of gratification to us to have the coöperation of the managers of various theaters in Cedar Rapids, Clinton, and Davenport, Iowa, and of the school superintendents and officials in these cities, through whom we obtained the observers who participated in this experiment. We are indebted to

Mr. W. H. Grubbs for painstaking and efficient assistance in devising and perfecting ingenious pieces of apparatus and for services as the experimenter's assistant while recording at the theaters and in the laboratory. We wish to express our gratitude for valuable assistance rendered in the reading of records by Miss Louise Arn and for clerical work efficiently done by Miss Shirley Jean Brooks.

W. S. D.
C. A. R.

Iowa City, Iowa
July, 1933

TABLE OF CONTENTS

LIST OF PLATES

LIST OF DRAWINGS AND GRAPHS

THE EMOTIONAL RESPONSES
OF CHILDREN TO THE
MOTION PICTURE
SITUATION

CHAPTER I

INTRODUCTION

THE object of this experiment was to discover the emotional effects produced by various types of incidents in the motion pictures on children and adults in a wide range of ages. For this purpose we drew upon several standardized techniques in use in the psychological laboratories for investigation of the affective life. This aspect of the human mind has for a long time resisted a direct frontal attack, partly because of traditional attitudes in regard to the emotions and partly because of the inherent difficulties presented by the emotional phenomena themselves. The traditional attitudes are rapidly being dissolved through the impersonal approach of the psychological laboratory, but the peculiar nature of the affective life had to be circumvented by certain procedures. The chief difficulty by way of analysis lies in the fact that the affective responses can not be directly attended to while they are in progress. Therefore, two groups of techniques have been developed: the procedure of impression, which requires the observer to report incidentally the pleasantness or unpleasantness of an ex-

1

perience during a well-controlled series of presentations; and the procedure of expression, which avails itself of the well-recognized principle that profound bodily effects accompany affective experiences. The experiment herewith reported falls under the second type of procedure. Whereever it was possible, verbal comments on the type of affective experience were also called for.

In recent years considerable attention has been given to what has been called the psychogalvanic reflex (PGR). There is plausibility in the argument by Lauer [1] that this is a misnomer and should be more accurately called the electro-biochemical response. While there is some question concerning the neurological mechanism of its functioning, there can be no doubt that it is intimately connected with the affective life when its form and appearance is such as to differentiate it from the effects of merely motor responses. In our practice there are two criteria which so differentiate it: (1) a period of latency from the onset of the affective experience to the first indication of its action, a period lasting approximately from 7 to 10 seconds; (2) the temporal course of its manifestation, generally arising very abruptly and subsiding gradually. There is also an additional element which has been demonstrated in our experiments and in many others outside of this laboratory, namely, that the extent of the response correlates directly with the intensity of the affective experience.

The galvanic response is measured through suitable electrical connections and apparatus, usually of the galvanometer type. It is manifested most definitely in those regions of the body that are richly supplied with sweat glands. It is, therefore, supposed that the electro-chemical changes in

[1] Lauer, A. R. Why not Re-christen the "Psychogalvanic Reflex"? *J. Exper. Psychol.*, 38, 1931, 369–374.

the sweat glands, mediated in turn by divisions of the autonomic system, are accompanied by electrical phenomena, which can be recorded through sensitive instruments. The electrical manifestation is, of course, so slight that it must be amplified many times before it can be recorded. This is done either through the electro-mechanical light-lever of the galvanometer, in which a beam of light is made to pass over a scale almost a meter in length, or more recently through the amplifying qualities of radio tubes with their accompanying circuits. The latter principle is used in the Hathaway apparatus.[2]

Another objective procedure for measuring the affective life utilizes the changes wrought in the circulatory system. This has also been thoroughly discussed and reviewed in the literature on the subject and, while there is still some uncertainty about its reliability, the procedure is useful within certain limits. The results obtained must not be overinterpreted but they do offer an indication of bodily disturbance. In our approach we have used it as a secondary source of measurement and have studied especially the increase in pulse-rate in connection with the motion-picture situation.

The underlying aim of this study, then, was to get both objective and subjective records of disturbances approximating an emotional nature during the motion-picture performance. The question arose as to what types of scenes emotionally excite children who go to motion-picture performances. We offer no thesis as to whether they should or should not be thus excited or within what limits a certain amount of excitement is salutary and wholesome on the one hand, or detrimental and unhealthful on the other.

[2] Hathaway, S. R. A Comparative Study of Psychogalvanic and Association Time Measures, *J. Appl. Psychol.*, 13, 1929, 632–646.

This is a subject which must be pursued by those who are experts in mental hygiene. But it is important to know actually what constitutes an emotional factor at the various age-levels and to what extent the emotional situations that are depicted are transferred to the child mind. Psychology has done much to correct the traditional notion that the child perceives what the adult perceives, but only perhaps to a lesser degree. We now know through numerous studies of child psychology that the mental processes are not qualitatively identical; that, for example, a thought process in an eight-year-old child is not in nature exactly the same as a thought process of an adult but that there are textural differences. In other words, the child is not a vest-pocket edition of an adult. In order, therefore, to get a true picture of what happens in the child mind, we tried to get an objective record of the bodily effect as well as indications of the actually felt experience from his own verbal reports. It must be admitted, however, that for the purpose of minute analysis children's reports are not in themselves wholly reliable. They serve merely as cues to aid the experimenter in the interpretation of his results. At the same time, they serve to correct any false impressions which he may draw either from his own reactions to the situation shown in the motion pictures, or from a more general account of the situation itself. In the sensory fields it is fairly safe to conclude that when a given tone of 256 ~ is stimulating the observer's ear, for example, he generally hears that tone. When an experimenter (E) [3] places a pistol next to the O's ear, he can not be certain that the O will have an emotion of fear. The O may have been conditioned to this situation in various ways. Recently one of the Es took considerable

[3] Henceforth, we shall use the conventional notations for the sake of simplicity: E for experimenter; O for observer. These are practically universally used in psychological literature.

pains to prepare some slimy spaghetti and chilled it to the temperature that would ordinarily produce a clammy feeling. However, a female O did not react unpleasantly at all when she was asked suddenly to place her hand in the jar with her eyes blindfolded. She afterwards told him that she had been in the habit of gathering "night-crawlers" for her mother for fishing purposes. In other words, in the affective realm it is not safe to argue from the situation to the affective response for the simple reason that we are now dealing not with stimuli but with situations that are perceived and, therefore, subject to conditioning in previous experience. It is a well-known fact that chemists working with H_2S not only get adapted to this usually unpleasant odor, but also consider it indifferently from the point of view of feeling. For this reason, as well as for the reason that E's own attitude should not be transferred *pari passu* to O without first scanning the record of O's verbal response, it is advisable to take the record of O's analysis of his experience, as well as to record through objective techniques the responses from his body.

As was indicated above, since the electrical techniques are also responsive to muscular movements we had to guard against these as much as possible, and in the cases where they would obscure the record these records had to be discarded. We feel, however, that on the basis of numerous other investigations conducted in the laboratory simultaneously with this particular study we were well on our guard against any extraneous circumstances or factors which might have vitiated either our records or our interpretation. We may, furthermore, state that as scientists we had no bias or prejudice in the matter, no particular "axe to grind." We were simply inquisitive and tried to get at the facts. It should also be noted that in order to be fair to the motion-picture situation both *E*s frequently attended motion pictures with and without their respective families, and one of the *E*s made a special effort to get into the atmosphere of production at Hollywood from several different angles. The periodicals which deal with this situation professionally were also carefully read and reviewed for this purpose. The point is here made because even scientists sometimes lean toward certain theories and are, therefore, unavoidably prevented from reaching disinterested conclusions. Great care was taken to guard against any such possibility of criticism.

With the advent of the talking picture, the illusion of reality in the theater is so great that to most of the spectators and auditors the presentations carry with them a deep emotional tone, especially in the case of children. In one particularly tragic scene the twelve-year-old daughter of one of the authors sobbingly said, "Daddy, is it really true?" There is no doubt that the motion pictures now have a strong emotional setting that induces in many instances profound bodily and mental effects. This study aimed to investigate the extent, intensity, and quality of these emotional effects. For this reason, while we perfected our techniques under laboratory conditions, we finally went out into the theaters to get the full effect of the "talking" situation and the social conditions at the regular performances.

CHAPTER II

HISTORICAL SURVEY

WE have already briefly sketched the history of the expressive method. We need now to discuss some of the antecedents of the galvanic response technique. The history of this technique has been repeatedly sketched in the psychological literature. [4]

As early as 1786, Bertholon investigated the changes in the resistance of the human body to the electric current. Throughout the early part of the nineteenth century a number of European physiologists became interested in various phenomena chiefly in relation to the human skin which revealed traces of electrical conditions. This was an age in which much attention was paid to what was commonly known as animal electricity or animal and personal magnetism. The topic had some implications in the direction of mesmeristic theories and the human body became in a certain sense an electrical machine which could be repaired through electrical means. Soon the question involved applications of muscular reaction, and by 1879 Vigouroux [5] suggested the diagnostic value of these changes in electrical resistance.

---

[4] Some of the more accessible references are: Landis, C. Emotion, I, The Expressions of Emotion, in *Foundations of Experimental Psychology*, Clark University Press, Worcester, 1929, pp. 488–523; Landis, C., and DeWick, H. N. The Electrical Phenomena of the Skin (psychogalvanic reflex), *Psychol. Bull.*, 26, 1929, 64–199; Landis, C. Psychology and the Psychogalvanic Reflex, *Psychol. Rev.*, 37, 1930, 381–398; Crosland, H. R., and Beck, L. F. Objective Measurements of Emotion, *Univ. of Ore. Publ.* (Psychol. Series), 1, 1931, 3, 133–202.

These publications cite hundreds of other related references on the subject,
[5] Vigouroux, R. Sur le rôle de la resistance electrique des tissus dans l'électrodiagnostic, *Comp. Rend. Soc. Biol.*, 31, 1879, 336–339.

In 1888 Féré [6] reported some work on the changes in electrical tension in the human body and referred these changes to atmospheric conditions, the vitality of skin tissue, and also to mental, including emotional, experiences. This type of investigation went on until 1892, when Féré published his "Pathology of Emotions." Just before this, in 1890, Tarchanoff,[7] a Russian physiologist, had begun to study the actual electrical energy manifested by the human body, or what has since been called the "endosomatic current," as distinguished from the techniques involving the outside source of electrical energy, or the "exosomatic current," to which the body offers a variable resistance. He suggested that this current was caused by the action of the sweat glands. While his stimuli suggested affective responses, he did not limit the phenomenon to emotional situations. His concept of the psychogalvanic reaction has some relation to the results obtained earlier by du Bois-Reymond. The matter was now in the hands chiefly of physiologists, neurologists, and psychiatrists.

In 1904 E. K. Müller,[8] a Swiss electrical engineer, brought these galvanic skin phenomena to the attention of Veraguth,[9] who conducted a series of experiments and brought them together in his book under the translated title of "The Psychogalvanic Reflex-phenomena," which was published in 1909. The records seem to indicate that he was the first to stress the effect of mental processes and more particularly the emotional experiences in this connection.

---

[6] Féré, C. Note sur des modifications de la tension electrique dans le corps humain, *Comp. Rend. Soc. Biol.*, 5, 1888, 28–33.

[7] Tarchanoff, J. Über die galvanischen Erscheinungen an der Haut des Menschen bei Reizung der Sinnesorgane und bei verschiedenen Formen der psychischen Tätigkeit, *Pflüger's Arch. f. d. g. Physiol.*, 46, 1890, 46–55.

[8] Müller, E. K. Über Einfluss psychischer und physiologischer Vorgänge auf das elektrische Vermögen des Körpers, *Physik-Med. Monatschrift.*, 1, 1904–1905, 212–214.

[9] Veraguth, O. Das psycho-galvanische Reflex-Phänomen, *Monat. f. Psychiat. u. Neur.*, 23, 1908, 204–240.

But the central thought was connected with psychoanalytical procedures. Jung [10] then proceeded to apply the technique to repressed ideas that were emotionally colored and used this technique in that connection. Gildemeister [11] has also done a considerable amount of work connecting the reflex to autonomic responses. Credit should also be given to Thouless [12] for his proposal involving a physical explanation of this phenomenon.

Since then there have been numerous studies in this country by Darrow, [13] who investigated the question of saturation; by Jeffress, [14] who tried to relate the two types of electrical phenomena; by Wechsler, [15] who also maintained that they were of the same general nature in terms of a counter E.M.F. and due to a change of polarization; by Bayley, [16] who investigated the emotion of fear using non-polarizing electrodes; by Patterson, [17] who analyzed the emotion of surprise in terms of the galvanic reflex; by D. W. Dysinger, [18] who related the method of impression with the galvanic reflex; and by many others too numerous to mention. One can not afford to omit, however, the work of Syz, [19] who has applied the technique to pathological cases, and the service of Landis, [20] who, in addition

[10] Jung, C. G. On the Psychophysical Relation of the Associative Experiment, *J. Abnorm. Psychol.*, 1, 1907, 247–255.

[11] Gildemeister, M. Über elektrischen Widerstand, Kapazität und Polarisation der Haut; II Mitteilung, Menschliche Haut, *Pflüger's Arch. f. d. g. Physiol.*, 219, 1928, 89–110.

[12] Thouless, R. H. The Causes of the Continuous Change of Resistance Observed in Psychogalvanic Experiments, *Brit. J. Psychol. (Gen. Sect.)*, 16, 1925, 5–15.

[13] Darrow, C. W. Sensory, Secretory, and Electrical Changes in Skin Following Bodily Excitation, *J. Exper. Psychol.*, 10, 1927, 197–226.

[14] Jeffress, L. A. Galvanic Phenomena of the Skin, *J. Exper. Psychol.*, 11, 1928, 130–144.

[15] Wechsler, D. Further Comment on the Psychological Significance of the Galvanic Reaction, *Brit. J. Psychol. (Gen. Sect.)*, 16, 1925, 136–139.

[16] *Op. cit.*

[17] *Op. cit.*

[18] *Op. cit.*

[19] Syz, H. C. Psychogalvanic Studies on Sixty-four Medical Students, *Brit. J. Psychol. (Gen. Sect.)*, 17, 1926–1927, 54–69.

[20] Landis, C. Electrical Phenomena of the Body during Sleep, *Amer. J. Physiol.*, 81, 1927, 6–19.

to several summaries, has investigated these phenomena during the sleeping period.

While the extensive literature reveals a mass of various interpretations of the galvanic reflex and a variety of interest on the part of the investigators, the better controlled experiments by Wechsler,[21] by Syz,[22] and especially those of Washburn, et al.,[23] indicate that the deflections are to a large extent correlated with emotional experiences. In the last set of studies cited, Os who were rated as emotional had greater galvanometric deflections when recalling emotional situations than those who were rated as calm, and the extent of the deflections correlated both with the degree of emotionality of O and with the intensity of the revived emotion as introspectively reported. These results confirm those reported from our laboratory and cited above (Bayley, Patterson, Dysinger, and Smith [24]). So far as the authors are aware, no experiments have been published which utilized the motion-picture situation as provocative of the emotional experiences. This study, then, opens a new field for experimental investigation of the emotions.

[21] Wechsler, D.   On the Specificity of Emotional Reactions, *Amer. J. Psychol.*, 36, 1925, 424–426.
[22] Syz, H. C.   Psychogalvanic Studies in Schizophrenia, *Arch. Neurol. and Psychiat.*, 16, 1926, 747–760.
[23] Washburn, M. F., and Pisek, F.   Galvanometer Experiments with Revived Emotions as a Test of Emotional and Phlegmatic Temperaments, *Amer. J. Psychol.*, 36, 1925, 459–460; Washburn, M. F., Harding. L., Simons, H., and Tomlinson, D.   Further Experiments on Directed Recall as a Test of Cheerful and Depressed Temperaments, *Amer. J. Psychol.*, 36, 1925, 454–456; Washburn, M. F., Rowley, J., and Winter, G.   A Further Study of Revived Emotions as Related to Emotional and Calm Temperaments, *Amer. J. Psychol.*, 37, 1926, 280–283.
[24] *Op. cit.*

CHAPTER III

PROGRAM OF THE STUDY

Our aim was to make a comparative study of the emotional and affective experiences aroused by the observation of motion pictures. The different age-groups were compared as they reacted to the same scenes in motion pictures. Sex differences and individual differences were similarly examined. Exhibitions in the laboratory were arranged to give opportunity for the study of considerable numbers of Os in the various age and sex groups. These studies were supplemented by exhibitions under actual theater conditions, with smaller numbers of Os.

The comparisons were made on the basis of the psychogalvanic response. The resistance of the body to a small electrical current was first measured, and the change in this resistance under the stimulation of the motion picture was then photographed by the Wechsler psychogalvanograph. The actual millimeter deflection of the response line was transposed into a percentage of the original resistance of the body in order to make the results comparable from one O to another. This transposition of millimeters into percentages was made by the calibration of the instrument. Comparisons were thus made in the study in terms of the percentage of the original resistance of the body which is changed under the stimulation of the motion picture.

The study assumes then that the psychogalvanic response gives a significant index of emotional experience. This assumption was further tested by showing the picture

11

the second, third, and fourth times to the same *O*s. The problem of this phase of the study was to find whether the change of bodily resistance decreased after the first showing of the picture. Verbal reports were called for as to the intensity of the emotional experience upon reshowing. For purposes of comparison, the pulse-rate was also recorded and counted during a part of the experiment. In this phase, the purpose was to add data concerning other physiological changes during the observation of motion pictures.

These objective results were supplemented by verbal reports from each *O* in the laboratory. The reports were designed to give indications of the emotional and perceptual experiences and to give suggestions for use in the interpretation of results.

OBSERVERS

In the laboratory a total of 89 *O*s were used. Forty-two of these saw both the two parts of *Hop to It Bell Hop* and the two parts of *The Feast of Ishtar*. Ages ranged from six years and four months to adults over 50 years of age. The number in each age-group was as follows: under 11 years, 16 *O*s; 11 to 12 years, 11 *O*s; 13 to 15 years, 16 *O*s; 16 to 18 years, 15 *O*s; 19 to 25 years, 22 *O*s; over 25 years, 9 *O*s.

An effort was made to get *O*s of good average intelligence to represent the various age-groups. Where intelligence quotients were available, children of 90 to 110 I.Q. were preferred. Where intelligence quotients were not available, the criterion of normal age-grade progress in school was used. The group averages were somewhat higher than normal. Out of 54 *O*s under 18 years, I.Q.'s of 27 are available, averaging 112. In the group over 19 years of age, chiefly college students and graduate students were used.

Under conditions of the theater, three age-groups were used: those near 9 years of age, those near 16 years, and those near 22 years. The two younger groups were chosen by normal age-grade progress in school. The 22-year-old group consisted of both college students and younger working groups. A total of 61 *O*s was used in the theater, 19 in the 9-year-old group, 21 in the 16-year-old group, and 18 in the 22-year-old group.

Apparatus

Our first experiments were conducted in a laboratory studio with an aluminum screen measuring $3\frac{1}{2}' \times 4\frac{1}{2}'$ mounted at one end of the room and an Eastman kodascope, Model A, projecting a 16-mm. film, stationed at the other end. On a table to one side stood the Wechsler psychogalvanograph.[25] The room was equipped with about a dozen chairs. Attached to one chair were the non-polarizing liquid electrodes which have been described in a previously published article.[26] These were used throughout the experiment.

The essential features of the Wechsler psychogalvanograph as modified in this laboratory are shown in Fig. 1 on page 19. The chief modifications consist in adding a vibrating steel bar (T_2) dipping in a mercury cup and in series with a small 2.5-v. flashlight. This was the timing device which took the place of the metronome, that is usually provided as an accessory to the psychogalvanograph, under the conditions of the theater. In the laboratory we used the metronome set at 90, as explained later under the section on procedure. But obviously in the theater the

[25] Listed and illustrated in the general catalogue of the C. H. Stoelting Company under No. 24, 201.
[26] Ruckmick, C. A., and Patterson, E. A Simple Non-Polarizing Electrode, *Amer. J. Psychol.*, 41, 1929, 120–121.

·metronome would have made too much noise. The theater timing device gave half-second intervals in the time-line on the moving film within the psychogalvanograph. Figure 1 shows the wiring diagram and the essential features in the recording apparatus. The dash line incloses the circuit for the galvanometer proper. It consisted essentially of a Wheatstone bridge, (W_s), one of whose arms was connected to the electrodes (E) into which O dipped the index and third fingers of his left hand, as is shown in Plates II and III. The wires led off from this bridge to a galvanometer (G), the reflected light from the mirror of which shone on a sensitive roll of film. The film used in the laboratory was the regular Eastman film, No. 122, $3\frac{1}{4}'' \times 5\frac{1}{2}''$, six and ten exposures to the roll; and in the theater verichrome film of the same size with ten exposures to the roll was used. The instrument also contained a motor (M), which drove the film past the aperture and derived its energy from the service supply (S), using 110-v. alternating current. This supply also passed through the primary of a transformer (T_1) from which the current was drawn for the lamp (L), interrupted by the vibrating bar (T_2) and produced thereby a time-line in half-seconds on the film.

Outside of this circuit, but with a galvanometer contained inside of the inclosed and light-proof box, was a second galvanometer, which received its impulses from another Wheatstone bridge (W_h). To the opposite poles of this bridge a carbon button was connected through two dry cells (3-v.). This carbon button served to record the pulse-rate and also respiration. It was an improved form of the electrical pneumo-cardiograph described and illustrated in detail in a separate article.[27] The device is illustrated in

[27] Grubbs, W. H., and Ruckmick, C. A. An Electrical Pneumograph, *Amer. J. Psychol.*, 44, 1932, 180–181.

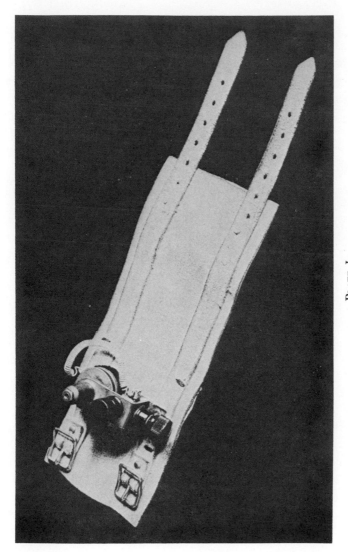

PLATE I

THE LEATHER ARM STRAP OF THE PNEUMO-CARDIOGRAPH

Plate 3. The improvement consisted largely of an adjustable leather strap, which was fastened around O's arm, and a coil spring, which maintained a uniform pressure on the skin at the point of application. The reflected light from the galvanometer in circuit with this system impinged on the same moving film. The function of both Wheatstone bridges was to balance the galvanometer and to bring its deflection to zero at the start. From the adjustment of W_s, the total ohms resistance of O's bodily connection between the two fingers could be calculated.

In addition to this apparatus with its accessories there was a signal system between the E, who took his station near O, and the assistant, who manipulated the apparatus and who, in the laboratory, operated the kodascope. The system was a two-way system operating a small flashlight which was painted dark except for a pin-hole aperture. This whole system was set up also in the theater but, of course, without the necessity of a projectoscope.

PROCEDURE IN THE LABORATORY

Since the laboratory exhibitions by means of the kodascope required 16-mm. films, the most adequate motion pictures available in this size were selected. The pictures used were taken from theater films and represented fairly well the theater product. These pictures were descriptively outlined and sections were chosen for recording O's reactions by means of the psychogalvanograph. Various kinds of situations were included in the sections chosen. A detailed outline of these parts of the picture was then made and identification symbols were devised in the form of dots of varying number. During the showing of the picture these identification symbols were transferred to the record film through the stimulus key attachment, making possible the identification of the exact point in the picture which was represented by any point on the record film.

O was seated in a chair with an arm rest to the left. The index and third fingers of the left hand were washed with 95% ethyl alcohol and wrapped above the first joint with adhesive tape. These fingers were then placed in the liquid electrodes, with the arm on the arm rest. During this period of preparation for the experiment, E made an effort, especially with children, to put O at ease by informal conversation. The procedure at this point was not equivalent from one O to another, since the problem seemed to be one of rapport. With a single exception, adequate rapport was established. Usually there was little difficulty in view of the anticipation of the motion picture.

The resistance of O was then determined. Resistance readings were taken each minute until there was no change for a period of approximately one minute in length. The light in the room was then turned off and the metronome was turned on. Time was allowed at this point for further deflections of the galvanometer and for adjustment. Most frequently there was no reaction to the darkening of the room or to the sound of the metronome. The latter sound merged with the noise of the kodascope itself during the showing of the picture and was only faintly discernible. A light shone through a transom at right angles to the kodascope light, falling on O sufficiently brightly so that E could easily observe gross movement. E remained quiet behind O during the showing.

After the showing of the picture, O was asked to report in answer to the question, "What were the exciting parts?" When this uniform question failed to elicit a response, other questions designed to call out responses were used, especially with the children. Individual scenes were seldom

PLATE II

THE LABORATORY THEATER

A youthful *O* is shown holding the fingers of his left hand in the electrodes. The psychogalvanograph is on the table, with the Kodascope on the stand at the back of the room.

mentioned by E to avoid suggestion; when they were mentioned, notation was made in the record of the report and the report must be correspondingly discounted.

In cases of romantic or erotic scenes, a report was requested. If it was not volunteered in answer to the first general question, "What were the exciting parts?" the further question was put, "How did you like the love-scenes?" If an adequate response was not given to this clear question, the attempt to get a report on such scenes was abandoned.

Not more than two 15-minute films were shown at a single experimental period. The two parts of *Hop to It Bell Hop* and *The Feast of Ishtar* were shown consecutively on the same day, with a few exceptions. Showings for children came chiefly after school hours, though the time of day was not identical for each O.

PROCEDURE IN THE THEATER

The pictures used in the theater were chosen almost at random. No effort was made to get extreme results from the more frightful pictures. The dates acceptable to the theater management, to school authorities, and to E and the assistant left rather small room for a choice of picture. The result was a fairly good sampling of current motion pictures.

The pictures were previewed in order to obtain an outline of the plot. Sections to be used for detailed study were chosen and incidents were identified by a series of symbols for transfer to the record film. In the theater, a seat was prepared with two special arms, the left one holding the liquid electrodes and the right one for the arm with the pneumo-cardiograph. E was seated in the row behind O, a little to one side, with the control board before him. The control board had electrical connections to the psychogalvanograph, governing the motor which moves the film, the stimulus key to the record film, and the movement record on the film. The apparatus was placed about 20 feet from E, in charge of an assistant who balanced the galvanometer, kept the record of resistances, adjusted the pneumo-cardiograph and the timing mechanism, changed films in the psychogalvanograph, and did other work in connection with the apparatus. A simple signal system connected E with the assistant.

The experiment was performed in the balcony of the theater in three of the studies and in the rear row of the first floor in another. Few patrons of the theater came to the balcony, keeping the social situation relatively constant. In *His Woman* the rear row of the first floor was used and the social situation was, therefore, not constant from one O to another. A block of three rows of seats was reserved, however, to prevent extreme differences.

The procedure in the theater followed the laboratory procedure closely. The cleaning of the fingers with alcohol, the taping of the two fingers, the resistance readings until the galvanometer was balanced all followed the laboratory practice. The pneumo-cardiograph was placed over the pulse of the right arm and that hand was guided, palm down, on to the arm rest. Instructions were simple, asking for as little movement as possible so long as the fingers were in the solution of the electrodes. While sections of the picture were being shown, which were not included in the study, the fingers were removed from the electrodes and a reasonable amount of movement was permitted. When the fingers were returned to the electrodes the instrument was balanced again as in the usual procedure.

The effort to get systematic reports of the experience from each O in the theater was abandoned. The physical situation made it very difficult and unsatisfactory, while

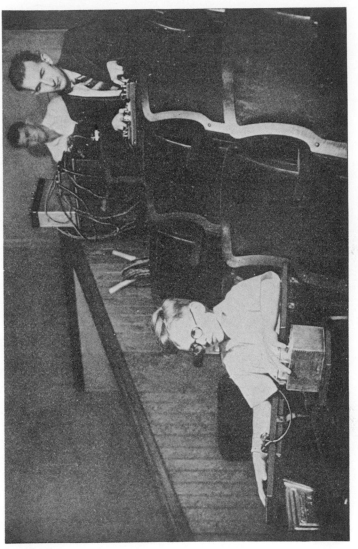

PLATE III

THE EXPERIMENT IN THE THEATER

O is shown holding the fingers of his left hand in the electrodes. The wrist-band of the pneumo-cardiograph is seen around the right wrist. The control board is seen at *E*'s position, with the psychogalvanograph
and other apparatus under the control of the assistant.

the time element added complications which led to the abandonment of the effort.

READING OF THE FILMS

For reading the films a reading box was prepared.   A small wooden box was fitted with a 5-watt bulb and a glass cover.   A millimeter scale was adjusted over the glass cover.   Magnifying the films through a reading glass, E was able to read the galvanometer line with ease and accuracy.   The readings in millimeters were transposed by table into percentages.   These tables were prepared by calibrating the galvanometer at all resistances from 4,000 ohms to 40,000 ohms, measuring the amount of resistance change necessary at each of these resistances to produce deflection of from two to thirty-six millimeters.

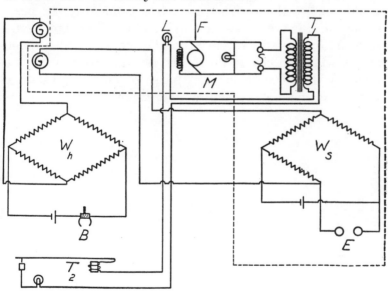

FIG. 1
SCHEMATIC DRAWING OF THE APPARATUS

In order to check the accuracy of the galvanometer readings, a second reader determined the calculations at 136 reading points. These results were correlated with the previous reading by E, with a result of .97 $\pm$ .004.

In reading the pulse records, 30 half-second time-lines were counted from the beginning of the reading point. The peaks of the curves were then counted and the rate per minute was taken as the reading. This result, contrasting with the galvanometer result, was relatively unsatisfactory. A large number of question marks had to be added to the tables, in order to express the uncertainty of the readers in the identification of the peaks of the curve. When the rereading was made for purposes of correlation the differences were found to be too large for accurate work. Upon reëxamination of the original results, the difficulty could not be solved. The problem is to identify the peaks of the heart curve on a slow-moving film. There are enough satisfactory records, reviewed in the section of this monograph which discusses the heart records, to give supplementary data concerning this phase of physiological functioning during motion-picture observation.

CHAPTER IV

GENERAL LABORATORY RESULTS

HOP TO IT BELL HOP

PART I

(The picture opens with a hotel lobby scene. A large bell hop (B) is then shown rolling a cigarette. A small bell hop (L) is shown blinking. He is about to sneeze, and just then tobacco is spilled out of B's cigarette, once, twice. B threatens L. L ties his shoes, getting one of B's shoestrings with one of his own. An oscillating electric fan is seen to be the cause of B's accidents with his cigarette. B turns it off [28]) as L completes tying the shoes. L sits up and sneezes away the cigarette makings. B grabs him by the neck and shakes him hard. L offers a cigarette which B snatches.

(In front of the hotel, a taxi stops. A pretty salesgirl gets out and enters the hotel. The clerk gives her the register to sign as he hits the bell for a bell boy.) L starts, but B pushes him back. B preens, takes a step and falls, tripped by the shoes tied together (1). B attacks L again, and the clerk demands that they go out to get the lady's baggage.

(B takes two suit cases out of the taxi, finds the trunks too heavy, and turns the job over to L. L takes four trunks out of the taxi with some flourish.) All the trunks are piled high on L's back, with B carrying the two suit cases. Precariously, L carries the trunks up the steps (2).

(The trunks are carried through the lobby to a door.) The door is too low. L stoops and B pushes. The top trunk is pushed off on to B's head (3). L drops the other trunks and tries to help B get the trunk unfastened from his head. The salesgirl sees a fireman's axe and gives it to L. L hits the edge of the trunk with the axe (4). He stands on a chair and hits the center. The trunk breaks in two and the axe is caught in B's head (5). It is removed with flourishes. L shows the axe to B and B throws a vase at L, missing him and hitting the clerk. The clerk goes after them but the saleslady interferes and B takes her suit cases to her room.

(A fat man [Fat] comes to the desk. He is sweating profusely and wiping his brow.) L appears on the mezzanine floor with a large bottle of ink. He spills it and the ink runs down on Fat. Fat wipes his forehead. The ink continues dripping. Fat wipes again, including his whole face (7), while his face and clothes become black. He turns to the clerk with the comment, "It's getting hotter," and the clerk is astonished (8). Fat sees himself in a mirror and begins to rave. The clerk steps out beside him to quiet him and calls to L above. L

[28] PGR records were not taken from the sections in parentheses. Numbers in parentheses indicate "reading points," *i.e.*, places where a mark was recorded on the film in the psychogalvanograph, for reference.

leans over and pushes the bottle of ink on to the clerk's head (9). L comes in fear to take Fat's suit case.

(Upstairs, B is leaving the salesgirl's room and Fat and L come to Fat's room. B is astonished by Fat's appearance and stands watching. Fat can not find his money but finally remembers it is in his small bag. He takes out a huge roll of bills while B looks on. Fat gives L a bill, advising him to buy a new face.)

L ties a string on the bill, placing it loosely in his side pocket and leaves the room. B takes the bill from his pocket; stands preening a moment as L leaves; the string tightens; L notices it and pulls the bill by the string. B notices a moment too late; starts after L, who runs into the elevator slamming the door on B, who falls hard (10). B watches the elevator indicator and runs to that floor. L escapes on the elevator to the first floor. Here B catches him, grabs him by the neck and shakes him up and down very hard (11). The clerk sees and stops it. (The salesgirl phones for a towel and the clerk sends L with instructions to give room 9 a bath.)

A drunken man is shown. He mistakes room 9 for his own, opens the door and sees the salesgirl exercising. He applauds and she slams the door (12). The room number swings around from 9 to 6. (The drunken man then enters room 6, where there is a dyspeptic old man. The dyspeptic throws him out, slamming the door. The number changes from 6 to 9. L comes to the salesgirl's door, sees the wrong number and goes to 9.) He enters, announcing that "The clerk told me to give you a bath." The dyspeptic protests, but L insists, pulls him into the bathroom, removes his bathrobe, picks him up (13) and puts him into the tub—pajamas and all. L takes him out of the tub, puts his bathrobe on, and leads him back into his room. The dyspeptic threatens to report L.

SUMMARY TABLE I
HOP TO IT BELL HOP, PART I

	D 1	D 2	D 3	D 4	D 5	D 6	D 7	D 8	D 9	D 10	D 11	D 12	D 13
F 6–10 yrs.													
Ave.	4.3	5.6	1.1	3.4	3.1	.7	4.9	1.8	3.0	4.1	3.4	1.6	.9
Range	2–6	2–12	0–8	2–8	2–5	0–2	2–11	0–4	0*–7	2–8	0*–8	0–5	0–4
No. cases	7	7	7	7	7	7	7	6	6	7	7	7	6
No. zeros	0	0	1	0	0	2	0	1	0	0	0	2	2
M 6–10 yrs.													
Ave.	4.4	9.0	3.9	4.9	4.3	4.9	3.9	1.0	3.4	7.0	3.9	1.0	1.0
Range	2–7	5–15	1–12	2–14	0–9	0*–10	0–8	0–2	0–8	0*–15	0*–7	0–2	0–6
No. cases	7	7	7	7	7	7	7	7	7	7	7	7	7
No. zeros	0	0	0	0	1	0	1	3	1	0	0	2	4

0* = slight response < 1
D = danger, conflict, or tragedy
S = suggestive or love scene

M = male
F = female

SUMMARY TABLE—*Continued*

HOP TO IT BELL HOP, PART I—Continued

	D 1	D 2	D 3	D 4	D 5	D 6	D 7	D 8	D 9	D 10	D 11	D 12	D 13
F and M 6–10 yrs.													
Ave.	4.4	7.1	2.5	4.1	3.7	2.8	4.4	1.4	3.0	5.6	3.6	1.3	.9
Range	2–7	2–15	0–12	2–14	0–9	0–10	0–11	0–4	0–8	0*–15	0*–8	0–5	0–6
No. cases	14	14	14	14	14	14	14	13	13	14	14	14	13
No. zeros	0	0	1	0	1	2	1	4	1	0	0	4	6
F 11–12 yrs.													
Ave.	6.0	2.8	2.4	1.8	2.5	1.4	6.2	2.5	3.2	1.3	3.3	.8	1.6
Range	2–10	0–6	0–6	0–5	0*–4	0*–5	1–17	0–7	0–7	0–3	0–7	0–2	0–4
No. cases	2	5	5	5	5	5	5	4	5	4	4	5	5
No. zeros	0	1	1	1	0	0	0	1	2	1	1	2	2
M 11–12 yrs.													
Ave.	3.7	10.8	4.6	3.3	2.4	1.0	5.0	2.8	3.2	7.0	2.3	1.7	1.7
Range	2–7	1–23	0*–9	0–10	0–7	0–2	2–15	0–8	0–10	3–12	0–3	0–5	0–4
No. cases	4	5	5	4	5	4	5	5	5	4	4	3	4
No. zeros	0	0	0	1	1	1	0	2	2	0	1	1	1
M and F 11–12 yrs.													
Ave.	4.5	6.8	3.5	2.5	2.4	1.2	5.6	2.7	3.2	4.1	2.8	1.1	1.7
Range	2–10	0–23	0*–9	0–10	0–7	0–5	1–17	0–7	0–10	0–12	0–7	0–5	0–4
No. cases	6	10	10	9	10	9	10	9	10	8	8	8	9
No. zeros	0	1	1	2	1	1	0	3	4	1	2	3	3
F 13–15 yrs.													
Ave.	1.0	2.3	1.0	1.0	.7	1.7	2.7	1.0	1.3	1.0	0	.3	0
Range	1–1	2–4	0–3	0–3	0–2	0–4	2–3	0–3	1–3	0–3	0–0*	0–1	0–0
No. cases	3	3	3	3	3	3	3	3	2	3	3	3	3
No. zeros	0	0	2	2	1	1	0	1	0	1	2	1	3
M 13–15 yrs.													
Ave.	1.8	5.7	2.5	2.3	1.5	1.0	3.0	3.3	1.3	2.0	2.6	2.0	.2
Range	0–3	2–10	0*–6	2–4	0*–4	0–2	2–5	2–6	0*–2	0*–2	2–5	0–6	0–1
No. cases	5	4	5	5	5	5	5	3	3	5	5	5	5
No. zeros	1	0	0	0	0	2	0	0	0	0	0	1	3

SUMMARY TABLE—*Continued*

HOP TO IT BELL HOP, PART I—Continued

	D 1	D 2	D 3	D 4	D 5	D 6	D 7	D 8	D 9	D 10	D 11	D 12	D 13
F and M 13–15 yrs.													
Ave.	1.5	4.3	1.8	1.8	1.2	1.2	2.9	2.2	1.6	1.6	1.6	1.4	.1
Range	0–3	1–10	0–6	0–3	0–2	0–4	2–5	0–6	0*–3	0–3	0–5	0–6	0–1
No. cases	8	7	8	8	8	8	8	6	5	8	8	8	8
No. zeros	1	0	2	2	1	3	0	1	0	1	2	2	6
F 16–18 yrs.													
Ave.	3.8	3.8	1.3	2.0	1.5	1.0	3.5	3.0	1.8	2.3	2.0	1.0	0
Range	0–10	0–18	0–4	0–9	0–4	0–4	0–6	0–11	0–3	0–10	0–7	0–2	0–0
No. cases	5	6	6	5	6	6	6	6	6	6	6	6	6
No. zeros	1	3	2	3	1	3	0	2	1	3	3	4	6
M 16–18 yrs.													
Ave.	1.5	4.0	2.5	0	1.5	2.0	3.5	0	0	1.0	1.5	5.0	0
Range	1–2	3–5	1–4	0–0*	1–2	0–4	0–7	0–0*	0–0*	0*–2	1–2	0–10	0–0
No. cases	2	2	2	2	2	2	2	2	2	2	2	2	2
No. zeros	0	0	0	1	0	1	1	1	1	0	0	1	2
F and M 16–18 yrs.													
Ave.	3.1	3.9	1.6	1.5	1.5	1.3	3.5	2.3	1.4	2.0	1.9	1.5	0
Range	0–10	0–18	0–4	0–9	0–4	0–4	0–7	0–11	0–3	0–10	0–7	0–10	0–0
No. cases	7	8	8	8	8	8	8	8	8	8	8	8	8
No. zeros	1	3	2	4	1	4	1	3	2	3	3	5	8
F over 19 yrs.													
Ave.	.4	.9	.3	1.0	2.0	1.1	3.3	.6	.5	.5	.5	.2	.3
Range	0–2	0–7	0–2	0–6	0–8	0–5	0–13	0–3	0–3	0–3	0–4	0–2	0–2
No. cases	8	9	8	8	8	8	8	8	8	9	9	9	8
No. zeros	3	5	5	4	2	2	2	5	3	4	5	6	4
M over 19 yrs.													
Ave.	1.7	3.3	1.2	.9	1.6	.6	1.7	3.5	.5	1.0	1.5	1.7	.3
Range	0–5	0–8	0–4	0–2	0–6	0–4	0–5	0–14	0–2	0–2	0–4	0–8	0–2
No. cases	6	7	6	7	7	7	6	6	6	6	6	6	6
No. zeros	1	1	2	2	1	4	2	2	2	1	1	3	3
F and M over 19 yrs.													
Ave.	.9	1.9	.7	1.1	1.9	.9	2.6	1.9	.5	.7	.9	.9	.3
Range	0–5	0–8	0–4	0–6	0–8	0–5	0–13	0–14	0–3	0–3	0–4	0–8	0–2
No. cases	14	16	14	15	15	15	14	14	14	15	15	15	14
No. zeros	4	6	7	6	3	6	4	7	5	5	6	9	7

HOP TO IT BELL HOP

PART I

INTERPRETATION OF TABLES

These tables are directly interpreted from the story of the picture. The series of "slap stick" accidents and tragedies is without ambiguity in the presentation. No love-scene is included; no depth of plot is involved. The humor of the incidents is more apparent to some Os than to others and there are perceptual differences of the simple type in this picture. These are discussed in the section on perception. The comparisons of the tables are, nevertheless, direct and relatively simple.

The composite age result shows the following averages: 6 to 10 years, 3.6; 11 to 12 years, 3.2; 13 to 15 years, 1.7; 16 to 18 years, 2.0; 19 years to adult, 1.2. The youngest group shows the largest deflection-index. With each older group, excepting the 13- to 15-year group, this deflection-index decreases. In terms of emotional experience this is interpreted to mean that the intensity of the emotional experience is greater among the younger Os.

HOP TO IT BELL HOP·

PART I

INDIVIDUAL DIFFERENCES

Among the youngest Os definite reaction is found in each individual record. This response is seen at different points of the picture, but there is no young O who gives an indifferent response pattern. Some give more extreme deflections than others, but all show substantial reactions at some points of the picture.

In the 11- to 12-year group the same observation holds true. Individual differences are seen in the differing points at which extreme deflections occur and in the greater consistency of large deflections among some Os.

In the 13- to 15-year group there is a wider range. One O (C 16) [29] gives eight zero readings, although there is one deflection-index of 6. The record contrasts with another O (C 54), who gives no zero reading. These are the extreme cases; the other Os show a consistent response between these extremes.

In the 16- to 18-year group, there are two Os who give low deflection-indices (D 13 and D 55), with a considerable group of zero readings. Such a record contrasts with the opposite extreme (D 51 and D 15), who respond quite consistently with large deflections.

Above 19 years of age the range is wider. One O (E 15) gives all zero and zero-plus readings except one, while another O (E 20) responds with readings, greater than one at all reading points except the first two.

HOP TO IT BELL HOP

PART I

SEX DIFFERENCES

The eighteen female and twelve male Os above 13 years of age give opportunity for sex comparisons. There are thirteen reading points. At one point, the averages are the same; at six, the female average exceeds the male average; at the same number, the male average exceeds the female. Consolidating the scores, the male average is larger than the female, as 1.7 to 1.3. This result suggests that the male response to such scenes is slightly larger than the female; the lack of consistency in this result makes the necessity of further data clear.

[29] The tables of individual deflections are included in the protocol of this study, which is on file in the library of the University of Iowa.

HOP TO IT BELL HOP
PART II

(The salesgirl phones again for a towel. L returns to the desk and the clerk demands that he go back "to bathe room 9," refusing to listen to his protest.) He goes to room 9, enters, grabs the dyspeptic man (1), takes him to the bathroom and plunges him into the tub of water again. L returns the angered dyspeptic to his room.

(The salesgirl phones to demand the towel. L returns to the desk. The clerk is angry as he commands that L return to room 9. L's argument is cut off and L returns.) He enters the room, slamming the door. The dyspeptic points and orders him out. As L goes after him the dyspeptic runs around the room. He jumps out of the window (3), lands below, gets up and runs off.

(B is in the lobby with a huge barrel of paint or whitewash. Fat is shown sleeping in bed. The drunken man is shown in the room above with a towel about his head. The water is turned on and is running over the floor. Fat smiles, as a sub-picture shows his dream of ocean bathing.) Fat stands with his hands in position for a dive. He stoops twice (4). The sea scene takes the screen; Fat dives from a rock (5) in his dream; the hotel scene returns; Fat jumps through the floor into the barrel of whitewash. He sits up and L comes to help him.

(B sees L and takes up the chase. L runs upstairs and hides in a large clothes basket, closing the lid. B runs up the steps in the search. A young Negress comes out of a room. The Negro cupid shoots an arrow and advises the janitor to "Go and get her." He kisses her as she puts some sheets into the basket. The Negress hits him in the face, knocking him over (10). The Negro gets up slowly as L, with a sheet over him, rises in the basket. The Negro looks furtively, then more directly, at the "ghost." His cap raises a foot above his head (11). The Negro runs, bumping into B at the corner of the hall. B kicks him, sees L, pulls the sheet from L's head, and then attacks him. L dodges and runs into a room. B falls against the door and then breaks in. L comes out of a closet wearing a costume of a devil. B is frightened as the devil chases him into the lobby, where a great disturbance is created (13). The clerk shoots, knocking L over and removes his head-cap. (Clerk and B are angry. The phone rings and the salesgirl demands a towel. As B is about to hit L, the clerk sends B to give the salesgirl a towel.)

(B leaves the elevator, passes Fat's room, thinks of the roll of money and conceives of a plan. He finds a waste basket, puts some paper into it, sets fire to the paper and throws it into Fat's room, as much smoke arises. Fat awakens from sleep, yells "Fire," runs downstairs, knocks down a man, grabs L's hand and the two go upstairs. B is shown searching for the money bag in Fat's room. L gets a fire-hose, gives it to Fat who falls. B still is searching for the roll of money. L turns on the water but none comes.) Fat and L look into the nozzle. As Fat looks again, L lifts Fat's foot from the hose and water squirts in Fat's face (15). Fat throws the hose to the floor. B is shown pulling a mattress from the bed where he finds the money bag (16). As Fat and L enter the room, B hides behind the door. When L and Fat pass the door, B tries to run out with the money bag. Fat grabs him, giving L a grip on the money bag. L tries to pull it away from B, fails, and then bites B's hand (17). B and Fat fight, B knocking Fat down (18). L runs up the fire escape with the bag. B is after him (19). L gets to the roof, sees B coming, runs on the roof, and climbs the flagpole. B comes to the foot of the flagpole and yells, "Come down." B begins to shake the flagpole and yells while the flagpole sways widely (20). L hangs on, B shakes harder and the flagpole falls over with L's end extending far out over the edge of the building (21). B raises the base of the pole. L falls many stories and catches himself on an awning frame. He swings here and then climbs into a girl's room (24). B looks over the edge of the roof.

(L holds the money bag and begins to explain to the girl. He gives her the bag as B enters. B grabs L as the girl leaves with the bag. B starts after her but L grabs him, knocking him over. B hits L and runs down the hall followed by L.)

The girl is on the roof, backing away from the stairway entrance. B comes and motions for her to come back. She backs up farther near the edge, at the

SUMMARY TABLE II
HOP TO IT BELL HOP, PART II

M and F	D 2	D 3	D 4	D 5	D 10	D 11	D 12	D 13	D 15	D 16	D 17
6–10 yrs.											
Ave.	.4	3.5	1.4	2.9	1.7	6.2	4.1	3.2	.9	.5	1.7
Range	0–3	1–11	0–4	0–7	0–4	0–20	0–10	0–9	0–4	0–2	0–14
No. cases	9	11	10	11	11	10	11	11	11	11	10
No. zeros	5	0	2	1	1	1	2	2	5	7	4
11–12 yrs.											
Ave.	1.6	4.4	2.4	6.0	1.8	3.3	2.2	4.5	2.3	1.3	2.3
Range	0–6	0*–8	0–6	0–10	0–4	0–11	2–3	1–8	0–5	0–4	0–7
No. cases	8	9	9	9	9	8	9	8	8	8	8
No. zeros	3	0	1	1	2	2	0	0	2	2	3
13–15 yrs.											
Ave.	1.3	1.6	1.3	2.0	0	.5	2.3	3.6	.4	0	.5
Range	0–7	0–7	0–5	0–4	0–0*	0–2	1–13	1–13	0–2	0–0*	0–4
No. cases	7	8	7	8	8	8	8	7	8	8	8
No. zeros	3	2	4	2	6	4	1	0	5	7	6
16–18 yrs.											
Ave.	4.2	4.4	7.0	5.3	1.8	2.8	3.6	3.6	.8	.4	1.8
Range	0–17	0–9	0–17	0–13	0–5	0–12	0–10	0–10	0–2	0–2	0–5
No. cases	5	5	5	4	5	5	5	5	5	5	5
No. zeros	2	1	1	1	1	2	1	1	3	4	2
over 19 yrs.											
Ave.	.4	3.0	1.6	2.4	.5	.9	1.2	1.5	.6	.1	.2
Range	0–3	0–13	0–16	0–12	0–5	0–10	0–5	0–7	0–7	0–2	0–2
No. cases	14	15	16	15	16	16	16	15	15	15	15
No. zeros	9	3	8	3	9	13	8	7	11	14	11

edge. L comes and is much frightened (30). As B runs toward her, she falls (31). L is frightened, hesitates and begins to run down the steps. He runs fast through the lobby, into the street and catches the girl (32).

B is caught on the roof by two policemen. He knocks them down but one gets up and fights. The policeman backs B to the edge of the roof where they fight (33). A glimpse is given of the ground below, just before the policeman hits B, knocking him from the building (34). Below stand L and the girl. B lands nearby and L kicks B twice and then chases him away (35).

(The girl congratulates L. She inquires what was in the bag.) L answers, "money," and opens the bag. With astonishment he removes a flask (36). The final moral is given, "Much ado about nothing," summing up the picture quite satisfactorily.

SUMMARY TABLE II—*Continued*
HOP TO IT BELL HOP, PART II—*Continued*

D 18	D 19	D 20	D 21	D 24	D 30	D 31	D 32	D 33	D 34	D 35	D 36
.6	7.0	3.5	2.9	2.1	2.0	4.0	1.2	3.4	2.8	.3	.2
0–3	1–	0*–	0*–	0*–	0–3	2–8	0–2	1–5	0*–	0–1	0–2
	17	9	7	5					14		
9	10	11	11	11	10	11	11	11	11	11	10
4	0	0	0	0	1	0	1	0	0	3	5
.6	5.1	4.6	4.3	3.4	4.8	3.3	3.1	5.7	2.6	.6	.7
0–2	0–9	0*–	1–9	0*–	1–9	0*–	0*–	1–19	1–6	0–2	0–2
		11		6		7	7	1			
8	8	9	9	9	9	8	9	9	8	7	7
2	1	0	0·	0	0	0	0	0	0	2	3
.3	3.7	2.7	2.3	3.4	3.0	2.9	1.0	4.0	2.1	.5	.3
0–2	0–	0*–	0*–	1–	0*–	1–4	0–3	0–7	0*–	0–2	0–2
	11	7	6	10	4				6		
8	8	8	7	8	8	8	8	8	8	8	8
4	1	0	0	0	0	0	2	1	0	4	4
2.6	5.4	6.2	5.8	6.0	8.0	7.6	4.0	5.3	2.5	1.8	1.3
0–2	0–8	0–	3–	0–	4–	3–	0–6	3–8	1–6	0–3	0–3
		10	10	11	12	10					
5	5	5	5	4	5	5	4	4	4	4	4
1	1	1	0	1	0	0	1	0	0	1	2
.3	3.2	2.7	3.2	2.2	5.1	4.0	1.3	4.6	2.5	.5	.1
0–3	0–	0–	0–8	0–7	1–9	2–7	0–8	1–	0*–	0–4	0–1
	29	10						10	8		
15	15	14	13	13	13	13	12	12	12	12	11
11	6	3	1	1	0	0	3	0	0	9	8

HOP TO IT BELL HOP

PART II

INTERPRETATION OF TABLES

Part II is a continuation of the story of Part I, featuring more extreme incidents of the same general type, a "slap stick" comedy. With the story of the picture, the tables of Part II are almost self-explanatory. No love-scene or depth of plot adds any complication to the interpretation.

The extreme average in the 16- to 18-year group is a result of weighting by 3 of the 5 *O*s, who showed large deflections at many of the points. If the cases were increased in number at this age, such extreme results would probably not be consistently seen.

HOP TO IT BELL HOP

PART II

INDIVIDUAL DIFFERENCES

From the age-groups under 13 years individual differences spread from extreme deflections down to moderate but nevertheless significant deflections. No indifferent responses are found.

In regard to the 13- to 15-year group the same statement is true. *O* (C 16) approaches an indifferent response more nearly than any in the younger groups. More zero responses appear, contrasting with the extreme responses of some of the group.

The five cases in the 16- to 18-year group offer a very wide contrast. *O* (D 15) gives quite extreme reactions, while D 13 gives 18 zero responses out of 23 reading points, with four substantial responses. There is probably a weighting in these cases toward extreme deflections.

In the 19- to 25-year group the extreme reactions become less frequent, the number of zeros on the tables increases. Rather large deflections occur,—often between series of zero or low reactions. Over 25 years of age the number of cases in the study is small, but the same general statements seem to apply to these Os also.

HOP TO IT BELL HOP

PART II

SEX DIFFERENCES

Among the group under 13 years of age the boys reacted more strongly than the girls, 2.9 compared with 2.5. The consolidated score includes all the reading points of the film. At 9 reading points, the female score exceeds the male; at 13 points the male score is greater, and at one they are the same.

Over 13 years of age the table gives the same result. The female average for all the points is 2.0, while the male is 2.4. Male scores exceed the female at 15 out of the 23 reading points.

THE FEAST OF ISHTAR

PART I

The picture opens with a view of the feet of the dancing priestess, Tisha, followed by a full length view (4). After the dance she lies on a divan (7) and her maids fan her. (A youth enters and kneels before her announcing the arrival of an expected visitor. She dismisses him, rises, and calls her maids to prepare the beauty aids.) She lies down again (12) and in a close-up stretches her arms above her (14).

(Jether, a country youth of wealth, is introduced. He enters the palace with awe and is admitted through luxurious curtains to the presence of Tisha. He approaches bashfully as Tisha responds boldly.) He slowly comes nearer to her. She reaches out with her foot, touching him on the hand (25). He takes her extended hand and walks nearer to her, sitting beside her. A servant peers through the curtains. She guides his lips to hers (29) and then turns her scant-

SUMMARY TABLE III

THE FEAST OF ISHTAR, PART I

	S 4	S 7	S 12	S 14	S 25	S 29	S 32	S 34	S 41	D 51	S 57	S 58	S 61
F 6–10 yrs.													
Ave.	2.7	1.5	1.8	3.3	.5	1.3	1.5	1.8	1.8	1.3	.8	0	.3
Range	2–3	0–2	0–6	1–4	0–2	0–5	0*–2	0*–5	1–2	0–5	0–3	0–0*	0–1
No. cases	3	4	4	4	4	4	4	4	4	4	4	4	4
No. zeros	0	1	1	0	2	1	0	0	0	1	3	3	2
M 6–10 yrs.													
Ave.	1.8	.2	.5	.5	.6	.7	.1	.7	.6	1.0	.2	.3	0
Range	0–5	0–1	0–3	0–2	0–2	0–5	0–1	0–2	0–2	0–3	0–1	0–2	0–0*
No. cases	4	6	6	6	7	7	7	6	7	7	6	6	6
No. zeros	1	4	5	4	4	5	5	4	3	2	5	4	5
F and M 6–10 yrs.													
Ave.	2.1	.7	1.0	1.6	.6	.9	.6	1.1	1.0	1.1	.4	.2	.1
Range	0–5	0–2	0–6	0–4	0–2	0–5	0–2	0–3	0–2	0–5	0–3	0–2	0–1
No. cases	7	10	10	10	11	11	11	10	11	11	10	10	10
No. zeros	1	5	6	4	6	6	5	4	3	3	8	7	7
F 11–12 yrs.													
Ave.	.4	.4	.4	.6	0	2.0	1.8	3.2	.8	.4	.6	.6	1.2
Range	0–2	0–2	0–2	0–3	0–0	0–5	0–5	0–8	0–4	0–2	0–3	0–2	0–6
No. cases	5	5	5	5	5	5	5	5	5	5	5	5	5
No. zeros	4	4	3	4	5	2	1	3	3	4	4	2	3
M 11–12 yrs.													
Ave.	1.3	.5	1.2	.7	.5	1.8	2.0	1.3	.9	1.5	.3	1.7	.5
Range	0*–2	0–1	0–3	0–2	0–2	0–4	0–6	0–2	0–2	0–3	0–1	0–3	0–2
No. cases	4	4	6	6	6	5	6	6	6	6	6	6	4
No. zeros	0	1	2	1	1	2	3	2	2	2	3	2	2
F and M 11–12 yrs.													
Ave.	.8	.4	.8	.6	.3	1.9	1.9	2.2	.8	1.0	.5	1.2	.9
Range	0–2	0–2	0–3	0–3	0–2	0–5	0–6	0–8	0–4	0–3	0–3	0–3	0–6
No. cases	9	9	11	11	11	10	11	11	11	11	11	11	9
No. zeros	4	5	5	5	6	4	4	5	5	6	7	4	5

SUMMARY TABLE III—*Continued*

THE FEAST OF ISHTAR, PART I—Continued

	S 4	S 7	S 12	S 14	S 25	S 29	S 32	S 34	S 41	D 51	S 57	S 58	S 61
F 13–15 yrs.													
Ave.	2.6	3.0	1.3	1.1	1.0	2.0	1.6	.7	2.1	1.3	1.0	1.3	.6
Range	0*–7	0–11	0*–3	0*–3	0*–3	0*–7	0–5	0–4	0*–9	0*–3	0–3	0–5	0–2
No. cases	5	7	7	7	6	6	7	7	7	7	7	7	7
No. zeros	0	2	0	0	0	0	1	2	0	0	3	1	1
M 13–15 yrs.													
Ave.	2.2	.4	.9	1.4	2.1	2.0	2.4	2.4	4.2	.8	2.9	1.8	2.0
Range	0–7	0–1	0–3	0–4	0–13	0–6	0–7	0–8	0–16	0–5	0–11	0–4	0–6
No. cases	5	7	9	9	8	9	9	9	9	9	8	9	9
No. zeros	2	3	2	4	3	2	2	3	1	3	2	3	1
F and M 13–15 yrs.													
Ave.	2.4	1.7	1.1	1.3	1.6	2.0	2.1	1.7	3.3	1.0	2.0	1.6	1.4
Range	0–7	0–11	0–3	0–4	0–13	0–7	0–7	0–8	0–16	0–5	0–11	0–5	0–6
No. cases	10	14	16	16	14	15	16	16	16	16	15	16	16
No. zeros	2	5	2	4	3	2	3	5	1	3	5	4	2
F 16–18 yrs.													
Ave.	3.5	1.2	4.0	2.6	3.7	6.0	2.5	7.8	4.5	3.4	5.2	5.2	4.0
Range	0–13	0–4	0*–14	0*–10	0–12	1–14	0*–9	1–15	1–9	1–7	0–16	0–12	0*–9
No. cases	4	5	5	5	4	4	4	4	4	5	5	5	5
No. zeros	2	1	0	0	1	0	0	0	0	0	1	1	0
M 16–18 yrs.													
Ave.	3.8	1.3	1.5	3.0	1.6	2.0	1.4	2.2	.8	1.8	.8	2.0	.4
Range	2–7	0*–5	0–4	0–14	0–4	0–4	0–5	0–7	0*–2	0–4	0–2	0*–5	0*–2
No. cases	6	6	6	6	5	5	5	5	5	5	5	5	5
No. zeros	0	0	1	1	2	1	1	1	0	1	2	0	0
F and M 16–18 yrs.													
Ave.	3.7	1.3	2.6	2.8	2.6	3.8	1.9	4.9	2.4	2.6	3.0	3.6	2.2
Range	0–13	0–5	0–14	0–14	0–12	0–14	0–9	0–15	0*–9	0–7	0–16	0–12	0*–9
No. cases	10	11	11	11	9	9	9	9	9	10	10	10	10
No. zeros	2	1	1	1	3	1	1	1	0	1	3	1	0

SUMMARY TABLE III—*Continued*

THE FEAST OF ISHTAR, PART I—Continued

	S 4	S 7	S 12	S 14	S 25	S 29	S 32	S 34	S 41	D 51	S 57	S 58	S 61
F over 19 yrs.													
Ave.	2.6	1.1	1.9	3.1	2.2	3.1	2.3	2.2	1.2	1.4	.2	1.4	1.0
Range	0–10	0–6	0–14	0–11	0–10	0–10	0–7	0–7	0–6	0–13	0–1	0–7	0–7
No. cases	9	9	12	12	12	11	11	11	12	12	12	12	12
No. zeros	3	3	4	4	4	3	3	2	3	6	5	5	7
M over 19 yrs.													
Ave.	2.5	2.1	1.1	2.1	1.1	1.7	1.3	1.4	1.1	.6	.3	1.3	.9
Range	0–5	0–9	0–3	0–11	0–3	0–11	0–4	0–9	0–4	0–4	0–2	0–4	0–3
No. cases	12	13	14	14	12	12	13	13	14	14	14	14	14
No. zeros	2	2	1	2	4	4	1	3	2	7	5	2	6
F and M over 19 yrs.													
Ave.	2.5	1.7	1.5	2.5	1.7	2.3	1.7	1.8	1.1	1.0	.2	1.4	.9
Range	0–10	0–9	0–14	0–11	0–10	0–11	0–7	0–6	0–6	0–13	0–2	0–7	0–7
No. cases	21	22	26	26	24	23	24	24	26	26	26	26	26
No. zeros	5	5	5	6	8	7	4	5	5	13	10	7	13

ily clad back. After hesitation he kisses her back and she reclines in his arms (32), where he kisses her lips (34). Another scene shows her displaying her wiles as she reclines on the idol, Ishtar (41).

(At a later time Jether enters the palace and sits on a divan. Tisha is engaged with an unseen lover who gives her a ring from behind a curtain, receiving a kiss as a reward.) She approaches Jether who kisses her hand, noting the new ring. They quarrel over the ring (51). (A jewel merchant tries to sell Jether jewelry for Tisha. Jether refuses to buy in spite of Tisha's plain request. The conflict reaches a climax as she throws the wanted jewelry on the floor.)

(A large hall is seen into which Pharis, a sea captain, comes.) Dancing girls are seen upon the stage. As a part of the act, they discard their capes (57) and then their skirts (58). They come onto the hall floor and dance around Pharis (61). Tisha's servant offers to introduce Pharis to Tisha. Pharis enters Tisha's palace, receives a welcome from her and drinks with her. Tisha's servant extends his hand in mute request for a reward from Pharis for the introduction but Pharis in answer spurts wine over his hand. The servant leaves as Pharis and Tisha drink.

THE FEAST OF ISHTAR

PART I

INTERPRETATION OF TABLES

The opening dancing scene with its beauty is classed as an erotic scene because of the scanty costume. Among the seven *O*s under 11 years of age a substantial average was found, chiefly the result of the reactions of the three girls and one of the boys. There was only one zero record, however, in the group. This was the highest average deflection found in this age-group in scenes classified as erotic. Among those of 11 and 12 years the average was much lower, with four zeros among the nine cases. The 13- to 15-year age-group showed a much higher average, with only two zeros out of ten cases. The 16- to 18-year age-group gave a much higher average again, with two zeros, both from female *O*s. The adult group responded with a lower average, with five zeros out of twenty-one cases.

Tisha lies down on the divan (7), giving another erotic scene. The groups of 6 to 10 years and of 11 to 12 years gave small response, with about half zero readings. The 13- to 15-year group showed a significantly high average, with five out of fourteen cases giving a zero response. Those of 16 to 18 years of age responded with a consistent, though not extreme, average of deflection. The group above 19 years of age gave a higher average and more zero responses.

At (12) the same erotic elements continue in the stimulus. The two younger groups showed small increases in average over (7). The 13- to 15-year age-group gave a small but consistent deflection. Among those 16 to 18 years of age, there was a larger and equally consistent response. Above 19 years the average deflection was smaller and the response was not quite so consistent. Tisha is seen stretching her arms upward as she lies on the divan (14), with the picture a close-up. There was a considerable response from the 6- to 10-year age-group. The 11- to 12-year group gave a much smaller average. The 13- to 15-year age-group gave a significantly larger response, with the 16- to 18-year group again larger, and the adult group smaller. With the exception of the 6- to 10-year age-group, this reaction pattern was typical of the results of many such scenes.

At (25) the backward Jether approaches the bold Tisha who finally reaches her foot to touch his hand. The erotic emphasis in the scene is unambiguous. There were small responses in the two younger groups, increasing responses at 13 to 15 years and at 16 to 18 years, with a decreased deflection average in the adult group.

At (29) the kiss is seen, with the advances clearly from Tisha. An ambiguity was reported from this scene which is important in the interpretation of some of the results. The servant peers through the drawn curtains just before the incident of the kiss. Youthful Os were especially prone to find danger in this spy, fearing lest he do some harm. To the adult O, the incident is simply one of others which announce that Jether has fallen into a love-trap, although some adult Os may share the child's perception. Although the scene remains classified as an erotic scene, the interpretation of the various response averages must take this factor into account. Such a classification is doubtless justified for most of the Os, especially for the older groups.

Tisha lies back in Jether's arms (32) to give an unambiguous love-scene. The index of deflection of those of 6 to 10 years of age was small with five out of eleven cases giving a zero reading. The 11- to 12-year age-group showed a much higher deflection index, with 4 zeros and 6 integral responses out of eleven cases. A small increase in average was given by the 13- to 15-year age-group with fewer zero readings. The 16- to 18-year age-group showed a decrease in average, with only one zero reading. One *O* of this group gave no reading at this point because the galvanometer line was thrown off the film by the violent reaction, a fact which can not appear in the tables. Above the age of 19 there was a large decrease in average, although the deflection-index is large enough to indicate definite response to the scene. The kiss follows (34), as Tisha reclines in Jether's arms. The 6- to 10-year group showed definite response, especially among the girls. The 11- to 12-year group gave larger responses, one of the girls giving a very large reaction. The 13- to 15-year age-group gave a much smaller deflection average, with a very large response from one of the boys. The 16- to 18-year group gave a greatly increased average, with a very large and an extreme deflection, with only one zero from the nine *O*s. The adults responded significantly, although the average is lower than in the preceding group. Tisha lies back on the idol (41), with her arms extended upward toward the face of the idol. The youngest groups gave small response. The 13- to 15-year age-group responded with substantial and consistent deflections. The 16- to 18-year age-group showed even greater consistency with a somewhat lower average. The adult group gave five zero readings out of twenty-six cases, with a lower average response.

The quarrel (51) is classed as a conflict-scene and showed little differentiation between age-groups. The two dance scenes (57 and 58) are erotic scenes. They gave small deflections in the 6- to 10-year age-group, larger deflections, especially at (58) for the 11- to 12-year age-group, increased response in the 13- to 15-year age-group, increased response again in the 16- to 18-year age-group, and sharply decreased response among the older *O*s, especially at (57). As the dancers surround Pharis with their act (61), similar comparisons between the age-groups appear.

The response of the age-groups to these erotic scenes can be compared by averaging the age reaction to each of the reading points except (51). The resulting figures represent an artificial combination of average indices from different scenes, so that the exact numerical significance of the figure can not be pressed. It does give opportunity, however, for gross comparison between age-groups. This comparison follows: 6 to 10 years, .85; 11 to 12 years, 1.0; 13 to 15 years, 1.9; 16 to 18 years, 2.9; 19 to 25 years, 1.60; above 25 years, 1.66. Above 19 years of age, there was practically no differentiation. In interpreting these indices in terms of the intensity of the emotional response to these scenes, the result showed small response up to the age of 12; a definite increase from 13 to 15 years of age; another definite increase from 16 to 18 years of age; and a large decrease among those of 19 or more years.

THE FEAST OF ISHTAR

PART I

INDIVIDUAL DIFFERENCES

Individual differences are marked. In the 6- to 10-year age-group, *O*s (A 54 and A 56) gave only one reading each above zero. At the other extreme, *O* (A 53), a boy of 9 years and 2 months, gave one zero reading. There are other *O*s in this age-group who showed significant response to this picture. There is little doubt that unchecked movement reached its highest point in this part of the study; yet such a consistent response can not be attributed to this factor. The point is an important one, since it concerns the age-level at which response to suggestive scenes or love-scenes is made. The average deflection-index of the age-group is low, yet there are Os who show significant responses. The range of individual differences includes almost complete indifference to the love-scene at the age of 9 and 10 years and also significant responses. The range of individual differences includes almost complete indifference to the love-scene at the age of 9 and 10 years and also significant response in exceptional cases at the age of 9 years.

In the group of 11 to 12 years a similar result was found. O (B 10) gave only zero readings, contrasting with B 13, who gave only 2 zero readings. B 13 is just one year and one month older than B 10. B 51 gave one significant deflection, with the remainder zero readings, while B 53 gave no zeros and only two responses of zero-plus.

In the 13- to 15-year age-group, O (C 57) gave zero readings at all points except (2) where the index is zero-plus, in contrast with C 58, who, although only 5 months older, gave only integral deflections. The range of the group is between these two extremes.

In the 16- to 18-year group, all Os show consistent response. Out of more than 125 reading points in this age-group, there are only 15 zero readings. Yet one O (D 55), gave seven out of the 15 zero readings, to give the one extreme of the range; D 11 showed a violent reaction, to give the other extreme. Most of the Os were well within the bounds of these extreme responses.

In the adult group, similar contrasts appear. Many more zero readings are found at this age-level, although a considerable number of large deflections are also found.

So there must be added to the statement of age-differences 'a general statement of individual differences. Within a single age-group, wider differences may appear than are seen between the averages of the two age-groups. The tendency of age-groups is clear, however, even in the individual differences.

THE FEAST OF ISHTAR

PART I

SEX DIFFERENCES

A study of the 12 points in this picture which are classified as love-scenes gives an approach to the question of sex differences in response to such scenes. The complicating factors in a few of these scenes, previously discussed, are disregarded in this review since they are of minor importance in the question of sex difference.

In the youngest group the female response exceeded that of the male Os in 10 out of 12 reading points, giving an average response of 1.3 for the former and of .5 for the latter. In the 11- to 12-year age-group, each sex gave an average of 1.1 at these twelve points, with the male average higher in seven points. The 13- to 15-year age-group gave eight points at which the male average was higher, giving general averages of 2.2 (male) and 1.5 (female). In the 16- to 18-year group the female average exceeded the male at 9 points, with a general average for the former of 4.1 and for the latter of 1.7. The 4.1 figure is largely a function of the deflections of one O who gave large and consistent responses through the picture. Above 19 years of age, the general averages compare as 2.1 (female) to 1.4 (male), with the former giving the larger reactions at nine reading points.

There seems to be a tendency for the female response to exceed that of the male. This is a function of the results from a few *O*s who gave rather extreme reactions, suggesting the possibility of a sampling error and the need of comparison with other results before a general conclusion would be warranted. But from other research work under way in the laboratory it appears certain that the female galvanic response is generally greater for many types of affective experiences than that of the male. This was not true, however, in the scenes of danger.

THE FEAST OF ISHTAR

PART II

(Jether is standing in the hall of Tisha's palace. As the Jewish servant leaves, Jether speaks to him, "Can'st thou not help me, Tola, I have great need of gold?" The Jew hesitates and Jether glances into the near-by room where Pharis is with Tisha. The Jew declines to give gold but offers loaded dice for the gambling hall. Jether protests that he is not a cheat but the Jew leads him to the gambling hall.)

They walk to a table where there is a group of gamblers. The Jew offers Jether's jeweled head-piece for examination by the gamblers and switches the dice (5). More bets are laid. Jether rolls and wins. New bets are placed and Jether wins again (12). A third time the bets are placed and the dice are rolled. A gambler grabs the dice (16) and accuses both of cheating (19). The Jew raises his hand and exclaims that he had thought this young man to be honest. Jether tries to explain but they drive him out. One gambler kicks him as he leaves (24).

(Jether appears at the palace of Tisha. Tisha is disturbed by his coming. He comes near her, accusing her bitterly and points to the captain in a bed near-by. Jether answers her sneer with a threatening touch on her arm (33). He grabs pottery from her hands (35), throwing the pieces on the floor. She calls for help (37) while he talks angrily. Three burly Negro slaves enter the room and two of them take Jether's arms firmly (40). She exclaims that she has long tired of him. He struggles to get loose but the two Negroes drag him out of the palace, with the third slave wielding a whip on his back (48). They throw him out of the gate where he lies in the street (50).

(Tisha is then seen at the bedside of Pharis. The maids raise the drunken captain. He smiles at one of the maids and Tisha calls for his attention.)

(It was a feast night in the city. The elaborate hall is shown.) The mob is eating at a most lavish table. The sea captain is shown in a close-up. He is feeding a group of girls but finally takes a meat roast and begins to eat it himself. Tisha is shown feeding a gourmand. Dancers come down the steps. The picture moves in a close-up of the tables, stopping at a rather extreme dance scene (59). During this dance a man takes a ring from a drunken girl's finger. The dancing group is seen in a rhythmic dance followed by wilder dancing, with the dancers landing in the laps of the feasters. They continue around the tables, with a close-up of one of the dancers (68). Tisha beckons a slave and commands that the gates of the temple be opened to all who wish to feast with her that night. The trumpeters announce and the crowds pour into the temple. Tisha approaches the goddess and leads a great crowd in worship. They bow low repeatedly. The face of the goddess is shown.

A fiery hand is seen writing on the wall in flaming letters (73). The writing

SUMMARY TABLE IV

THE FEAST OF ISHTAR, PART II

M and F	D 5	D 12	D 16	D 19	D 24	D 32	D 35	D 37	D 40
6–10 yrs.									
Ave.	1.9	1.7	1.8	.7	2.4	1.4	1.6	.7	2.7
Range	0*–4	0–9	0–4	0–2	0*–6	0–5	0–5	0–3	0–8
No. cases	9	13	13	13	12	12	12	12	12
No. zeros	0	3	2	4	0	2	3	5	2
11–12 yrs.									
Ave.	2.4	2.9	2.2	1.0	3.2	1.4	.9	1.4	2.3
Range	0–6	0*–9	0*–7	0–3	0–7	0–5	0–2	0–4	0–7
No. cases	7	9	9	7	9	10	10	10	10
No. zeros	1	0	0	4	1	2	2	3	2
13–15 yrs.									
Ave.	1.4	2.9	1.6	.6	3.4	.9	.7	.5	3.9
Range	0–6	0–11	0–5	0–8	0–7	0–5	0–2	0–2	0–28
No. cases	9	15	15	15	15	15	15	15	15
No. zeros	3	1	1	4	1	6	6	6	2
16–18 yrs.									
Ave.	2.0	2.2	2.6	2.7	3 6	2.6	1.3	1.7	4.4
Range	0–7	0–7	0–8	0–8	0–8	0–7	0–3	0–6	0–13
No. cases	12	11	11	10	11	11	11	11	12
No. zeros	2	3	2	1	1	2	1	3	2
over 19 yrs.									
Ave.	.6	1.2	1.2	.3	1.3	.7	.7	.4	1.0
Range	0–5	0–8	0–6	0–3	0–7	0–3	0–8	0–2	0–7
No. cases	21	22	21	20	21	21	22	23	23
No. zeros	9	11	6	8	7	9	8	10	8

is translated into English (75) giving a warning of immediate punishment. Lightning fells the idol (78). The mob begins to run. A close view is given. Chariots seem to pass forward over the spectators. Elephants, oxen and sheep are seen running (84). Various scenes show crowds running and panic in the buildings. Threatening clouds are seen above. Lightning strikes and buildings fall on many people (93). The banquet hall collapses on many of the mob (94). Clouds are seen again and fire rains from the heavens. Burning buildings, mobs in panic, and a rain of fire follows. The earth finally opens and swallows up the mob.

SUMMARY TABLE IV—*Continued*

THE FEAST OF ISHTAR, PART II—*Continued*

D 48	D 50	? 59	S 68	D 73	D 75	D 78	D 84	D 93	D 94
3.1	1.1	.8	1.5	1.9	.6	.9	1.2	2.0	1.0
0–7	0–4	0–6	0–	0–9	0–2	0–8	0–6	0–6	0–4
			10						
13	13	13	12	13	13	13	13	10	9
1	2	3	5	1	4	3	4	2	2
2.3	1.7	1.2	.6	1.8	1.0	1.1	1.5	1.1	2.6
0–5	0–4	0–5	0–2	0*–	0–3	0–3	0–5	0–5	0–
				5					11
10	10	10	10	10	10	9	10	9	9
1	2	4	6	0	3	2	2	0	1
2.1	1.5	1.6	1.6	1.8	.4	1.1	1.6	3.2	1.7
0–4	0–4	0–5	0–6	0–6	0–2	0–5	0–5	0–	0–9
								16	
15	15	15	14	15	15	15	15	14	12
1	2	4	6	4	5	3	5	1	1
3.0	1.9	2.7	3.1	2.0	1.0	1.7	2.2	2.1	1.9
0–8	0–7	0–6	0–	0*–	0*–	0–4	0–7	0*–	1–3
			10	5	4			5	
11	11	10	11	11	11	11	10	9	8
1	2	0	1	0	0	1	1	0	0
1.0	1.4	.8	1.1	.6	.6	.6	.7	1.2	1.1
0–6	0–4	0–3	0–6	0–5	0–5	0–2	0–4	0–3	0–3
22	22	22	23	22	21	22	20	18	17
10	8	8	7	7	8	6	10	6	6

THE FEAST OF ISHTAR

PART II

INTERPRETATION OF TABLES

From (5) to (24) the reading points are from the gambling scene in which Jether has been prompted to cheat by the Jew. The dice are switched (5). This incident showed a considerable reaction from each age-group except the adult, among whom the responses were small. The highest average was from the 11- to 12-year age-group. Few zero readings are found except among the adults. The dice are thrown the second time (12). The same general result was given at this point. The third throw is made (16). Deflection-indices gave similar averages again, the largest change being the decrease at the 13- to 15-year age-level. The gamblers grab the dice and accuse Jether and the Jew of cheating (19). Averages decreased and the number of zeros increased except at the 16- to 18-year age-level. Jether is thrown out of the building rather roughly (24). All averages increased sharply at this point and the number of zeros decreased correspondingly.

From (32) to (50) Jether quarrels violently with Tisha and is cruelly thrown out of her palace. He argues with her in anger (32). There was a considerable deflection at this point, although it was not so large as in the preceding reading point. The smallest average and the most zeros are found in the adult group. The 13- to 15-year group gave a smaller average in this scene than at other points where the incidents seem to be similar. Jether grabs two pieces of pottery out of Tisha's hands and dashes them to the floor (35). Averages dropped here except among the youngest Os. Tisha then calls for her guards (37). Responses varied quite widely at this point, although the averages are not large. Two burly Negroes grab Jether firmly (40). All averages increased, with the highest point reached in the 16- to 18-year group and the lowest point in the adult group. There were few zero responses except among the adults. Tisha's guards drag Jether out, whipping him as they go (48). Averages remained high, although they were not so high as in the preceding reading point. Except among adults, there were almost no zero readings. Jether is thrown to the road outside of the gate of the palace (50). Averages remained substantial, although they decreased among each age-group except the adult.

Scenes are shown which depict revelry and debauchery at a banquet in honor of the goddess Ishtar. At (59) a dancer is shown in a rather extreme dance at the same time that the theft of a ring from a drunken girl is shown. It is an ambiguous point; deflections may be to either of these focal points of the stimulating situation. Verbal reports which mention one or the other of these incidents are interesting in their identification of the phase of the situation which was noted. A technique for investigating personality trends through such a perceptual tendency is suggested by this result and may be worth careful investigation. In response to questioning some Os did not recall the theft of the ring, while other Os reported it as quite exciting.

Another dance is shown (68) which is classed as an erotic scene. Os of the youngest group gave a comparatively large response; the other deflection-indices are typical of such scenes in general.

The remaining reading points are from the destruction of the wicked city. Lightning, falling buildings, and fleeing mobs abound to produce a spectacular series of incidents. The film at this point is colored in red, adding to the effect.

Deflections were not so high as might be expected from such scenes. The record raises the question whether the observation of such spectacular scenes elicits as great an emotional response as would be the case in connection with more personal tragedies. No character of the preceding part of the picture is easily identified in this section. It is quite impersonal.

The warning hand appears (73). Deflections were highest in the age-groups of 6 to 10 years and of 16 to 18 years. The English translation of the flaming words appears (75). Deflection averages were much lower. A flash of lightning fells the heathen idol (78). Averages were somewhat higher. Elephants, oxen, and sheep are seen running among the people (84). Averages increased again with the highest point reached among the 16- to 18-year group and the lowest among the adults. Buildings fall on many people (93) and the banquet hall collapses on a part of the mob (94). Averages were not large at these points.

In consolidating the averages of each age-level for the scenes of tragedy, conflict, and danger, the following result was obtained: 6 to 10 years, 1.6; 11 to 12 years, 1.8; 13 to 15 years, 1.7; 16 to 18 years, 2.3; adult, .9.

THE FEAST OF ISHTAR

PART II

INDIVIDUAL DIFFERENCES

In the youngest group a considerable range appears on the individual tables, from A 14, who showed all readings of unity or above, to A 16, who showed 16 zeros and no readings of unity or above. This is a wide range, although most of the Os showed some zero, some zero-plus, and some readings of unity or above.

In the 11- to 12-year group a range appeared that is almost as wide. B 52 showed all responses of unity or above, while B 10 showed four such reactions, four zero-plus reactions, and ten zeros. Most responses were clearly between these extremes.

The range continues as wide among the 13- to 15-year Os. C 16 gave all zero reactions. C 58 gave all responses of unity or above. Most deflections were clearly between these extremes.

The range is slightly more narrow in the 16- to 18-year group. The least response was given by D 13 with three reactions of unity or above, nine zero-plus, and seven zero readings. D 50 gave all readings of unity or above, as did also D 53. There are many readings of unity or above in the age-group, with few zero readings.

There are many more zero readings in the adult group and no O who gave all responses of unity or above. The range is still quite wide, however, from Os (E 22 or E 13) at the extreme of small responses to O (E 50) at the opposite extreme.

THE FEAST OF ISHTAR

PART II

SEX DIFFERENCES

Among the Os of 12 years or younger there were no apparent sex differences. Out of the nineteen reading points the female average is the larger at seven points; the male average is the larger at nine points; and the figures are the same at three points. Averaging them, however, each gives a composite score of 1.6. The same relationship is true when the two points are eliminated which may be perceived as suggestive scenes.

Sex differences in this film are suggested among the 13- to 15-year age-group. Out of the nineteen reading points the male average is the larger at fourteen points, the female at three points, with the figures the same at two points. The consolidated averages give 1.3 for the girls and 2.0 for the boys.

Much the same difference appeared at the 16- to 18-year age-level. At fourteen reading points, the male score exceeds that of the female in average, while the opposite is true at four points. One point shows the same reading in both groups. In the consolidated average, the male response exceeds the female as 2.7 to 2.0. With the elimination of the two erotic scenes, this difference would be slightly less, although the same essential fact would remain.

In the adult group a similar result was found. The male average exceeds the female at fourteen reading points, while the opposite is true at eight points. Two results are the same. In consolidated average the female result is .6, while the male is 1.1. The result in the latter group would be somewhat less if the two suggestive points were removed although the change would be slight.

SUMMARY TABLE V
THE IRON MULE

	D 1	D 2	D 3	D 4	D 5	D 6	D 7	D 8	D 9
M and F 6–12 yrs. Ave.	5.2	3.6	3.5	5.7	3.5	2.1	6.6	6.0	2.6
Range	2–13	1–10	0–12	0–16	1–8	0–5:4	2–16	1–12:9	0–9
No. cases	5	7	10	10	8	10	9	8	10
M and F over 19 yrs. Ave.	4.2	2.4	1.2	1.1	1.0	.2	.8	.4	.8
Range	0–13	0–7	0–6	0–8	0–6	0–1	0–2	0–2	0–3
No. cases	5	11	10	10	8	10	10	9	9

THE IRON MULE

This is a humorous sketch taking its material from the period of the first railroads. After seeing the passengers get on the train, with several funny incidents, the conductor sits on the coachman's seat at the back, blows his horn for the train to start, and falls off backwards when it does start (1). They approach a tunnel and the engineer takes the smokestack off, climbs up the hill with it, runs fast over the hill (2), and meets the train at the other end of the tunnel. They come to a river, tie heavy logs to the sides of the train, pull into the water (3) and row rapidly down the stream (4). A horseman ties his horse to the train and hops a ride. The horse balks and stops the train. An exciting incident follows in which they try to induce the horse to move (5). The engineer joins a group of gamblers who are using the engine wheel as a roulette-wheel. A woman dramatically grabs her husband from among the culprits (6). The conductor unties the balky horse, talks a minute and the train runs away (7). A chase follows, featuring the falling of an old couple (8, 9, and 10).

Indians are seen piling logs on the track ahead (12). The engineer has found a bicycle and is riding hard to catch the train, when he falls off head over heels (13). The train hits the log pile (14). The Indians shoot arrows at the passengers (15). A pretty girl, who is framed in an open coach door, narrowly escapes a large bunch of arrows (16).

The engineer arrives and is splitting wood to start the fire. An Indian creeps up. The engineer grabs his tomahawk, kills the Indian (17), and chops wood with his new weapon. One passenger is chased by an Indian, hands the Indian his wig (19 and 20), and escapes. The Indian is angered to find that the wig came from Sears, Roebuck & Co. (21). The train is ready to pull away but a coupling breaks, leaving passenger cars behind (22). The passengers run and catch the engine, where they are shown as the picture ends.

SUMMARY TABLE V—*Continued*

THE IRON MULE—*Continued*

D 10	D 12	D 13	D 14	D 15	D 16	D 17	D 19	D 20	D 21	D 22
6.0	5.0	5.0	3.6	11.3	7.3	7.3	9.8	6.4	4.0	16.2
0–	0–	1–	0*–	0*–	1–	0*–	0*–	0–	0–	0*–
25	14	13	8	21:36	17	20	27	16	14	21:15
9	6	6	5	6	7	6	4	5	4	5
.9	.2	1.6	.3	.7	.1	1.0	.3	1.6	2.5	.1
0–2	0–	0–	0–3	0–6	0–1	0–2	0–1	0–8	0–7	0–1
	1:1	12								
9	10	10	10	10	8	8	8	8	8	8

THE IRON MULE

INTERPRETATION OF TABLES

This is a humorous film, picturing a series of pseudo-accidents and dangers. It was used in the preliminary stages of this study. The records afford a comparison of *O*s under 13 years of age with those over 18 years. The humor of the picture caused laughter sometimes during the showings and one can not be sure how much of this movement was effectively checked out of the readings. Some of the averages are heavily weighted by large individual deflections. The major point of this study is clear, however, that such scenes give much larger deflections among the younger than among the older *O*s. This is true in cases which gave little movement as well as in the other cases, and the verbal reports, because of their character and the enthusiasm with which they were given, point to the same conclusion.

CHAPTER V

SPECIAL LABORATORY RESULTS

RESHOWING TECHNIQUE

IF the major assumption of the validity of the psycho-galvanic technique is justified in this study a reshowing of the motion picture ought to show a decrease in the index of deflection. *O*s reported decreased emotional intensity. A situation which on first showing seems dangerous loses some of its emotional intensity when previous observation has given the assurance of a happy ending. Such a statement might not be true in the presentation of the more profound tragedies of life and is probably not true of love-scenes. Yet it is reported, and it surely would be expected in the pseudo-tragedies so frequently seen in motion pictures. The fall of a girl from a building, for example, might rouse considerable emotion but it would not be so intense after one knew that the companion of the girl would run down the steps of the building and catch her before she landed.

Part II of *Hop to It Bell Hop* was chosen for this test of the technique. It is characterized by pseudo-tragedies which have, without exception, happy endings. Two tests were made of other pictures: Part I of *Hop to It Bell Hop* and Part I of *The Feast of Ishtar*. The time which intervenes between the reshowings, indicated on the table, is essential to the validity of this technique.

In interpreting these tables one notes that there were 64 increases in the deflection-index, 90 points without

51

change, and 120 decreases. Adding the indices in each
class there were total increases of $90\frac{1}{2}$ and total decreases
of 232. This addition counts a change from 0 to 0* as
$\frac{1}{2}$. Two reshowings are included which had an interval of
more than five months between the showings. In these
two cases there were 11 increases in deflection-index, 6
points without change, and 10 decreases. All of the increases came from one of these Os, A 54; in adding these
indices, the increases total 19 while the decreases total
$15\frac{1}{2}$; in the second case, A 55, the decreases total $15\frac{1}{2}$.
Eliminating these two cases and using only the reshowings
which were less than two weeks apart, the total increases
are $71\frac{1}{2}$, while the total decreases are 201. Such results
would seem strongly to support the major assumption of
the study.

The comparison of the pattern of response on the record
film does not lend itself well to quantitative formulation,
although a striking result is seen. The pattern of response
in reshowings is similar to the first film record in a sense
that two film records are not normally alike. Samples of
film records are included (Figs. 2, 3, 4, 5) to show this relationship and to contrast it with other records selected
by random choice. In examining these records allowance
must be made for the variation in the speed of the
moving film which causes some records to be longer than
others. This parallelism is clear enough to suggest that
the experience in second showings, although less intense,
has much in common with the experience upon the first
showing.

The reshowing of *The Feast of Ishtar, Part I*, was suggested
by large reactions from one 12-year-old girl, to see whether
her deflection-index would decrease. The table is included,
showing a considerable decrease.

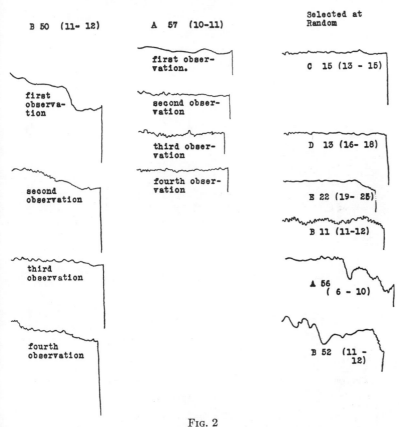

B 50 (11- 12) A 57 (10-11) Selected at Random

first observation.

C 15 (13 - 15)

first observation

second observation

second observation

third observation

D 13 (16- 18)

fourth observation

E 22 (19- 25)

B 11 (11-12)

third observation

A 56 (6 - 10)

fourth observation

B 52 (11 - 12)

FIG. 2

THE GALVANOMETRIC RESPONSE IN RESHOWINGS

These illustrations compare the patterns of response at the same point in the laboratory picture *Hop to It, Bell Hop, Part II*. The tracings of record fi ms from B 50 and A 57 show response patterns from the reshowing technique. Those selected at random are all first showings. Allowance must be made for differences in resistance and in the speed of the record film; yet the point is illustrated that the pattern of response in reshowings carries a similarity through all of the record films.

RESHOWING TECHNIQUE TABLES VI
HOP TO IT BELL HOP, PART II

	1	2	3	4	5	10	11	12	13	15	16
B–50 (Dates)											
4–14–31	0	0	3	2?	9	0	?	1		0	0
4–15–31	X	0	1	5	4	1	2	6		0	0
4–24–31	X	0	0	1	4	0*	0*	3		0	X
4–28–31	1:1	0*	2	2	4	3	1	3		1:1	0*
A–57 (Dates)											
4–20–31	X	0*	2	2	1	0	?	3		0	0
4–20–31	X	0	0*	0*	1	0	0	1		0	0
4–24–31	X	1	0*	0*	0*	0	1	1		0	0
4–28–31	0*	1	0*	0	0*	1	0	0*		0	0
D–13 (Dates)											
2–18–31	X	0	0	0	0	0	0	0	0	0	0
2–23–31	0	0	0	0	0	0	0	0	0	0	0
A–54 (Dates)											
11–10–30	0*	0*	3	1	2	1	5	10	2:4	1	0
4–25–31	0	0*	4	4	4	0	8	11	X	2	1
4–25–31	0*	0	0*	1	1	0	3	4	6	0	0*
B–13 (Dates)											
4–16–31	X	2	7	4	5:3	4	6	6		4	1
4–21–31	0*	0*	6	4	2	2	2	4:M		1:M	0*
A–55 (Dates)											
11– 8–30	X	3	3	2	3	0*	6	3	3	2	2
4–25–31	1	2	3	1	1	0	X	5		0*	0*
A–15 (Dates)											
4–17–31	X	X	2	4	0*	?	8?	0	0	0	0
4–27–31	X	1	4	3	2	2	4	2		0*	0*
4–27–31	X	0*	2	4	0*	4	4	2		0*	0*

RESHOWING TECHNIQUE TABLES VI—*Continued*
HOP TO IT BELL HOP, PART II—*Continued*

17	18	19	20	21	24	30	31	32	33	34	35	36
0	0	8	5	8	3:3	6	3	3:2	6	3	0	0
0	3	6?	4	2	2	4	3	0*	4	3	0	0
0	0	0*	2	5	2	2	3	0*	4	1	0*	0*
0	0	1	0*	5	2	2	2	0*	2	2	0*	0*
0	0*	4	3	4	2:1	3	3 | 5	0	2	0*	0*	0
1	1	2	3:2	3	1			1	0*	2	0	0
0*	0*	0*	2	2	1		0*	1	0*	0*	0	2?
1	0	0*	0*	2	0		0*	0*	2	0*	0	0*
0	0	0	0	7	0	4	3	0	3	1	0	0
0	0	1	0	1	0*	2	2	0	0*	0	0	0
1	X	9	6	4	5	3	4	1	5	4:10	0*	0*
1	4	8	6	8	3	4	5	2	2	6	X	X
1	?	8?	3?	?	?	6	7	1	?	?	?	?
1?	1?	6?	5?	3?	2	2 | 3		2	2	?	?	?
1	1	3:M	2:M	1	0*	4		1	4	1	?	2
X	X	X	2	2	2	2	2	2	2	2	0	0*
1	2	1	1	2	1	1	2	1	0*:M	0*	X	X
0	0	11	4	7	3	0	7	2	4	2	0*	0
0*	0*?	6	3	4	3	4	3	0	2	2	0	0*
0*	0*	7	3	0*	3	4	3	0*	3	1:M	0*	0*

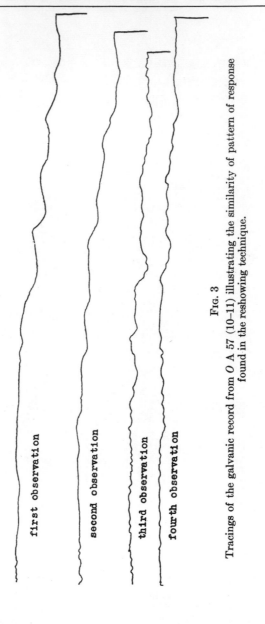

first observation

second observation

third observation

fourth observation

FIG. 3

Tracings of the galvanic record from *O* A 57 (10–11) illustrating the similarity of pattern of response found in the reshowing technique.

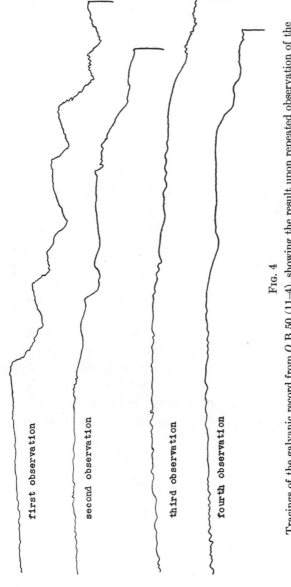

first observation

second observation

third observation

fourth observation

Fig. 4

Tracings of the galvanic record from *O B 50* (11–4), showing the result upon repeated observation of the same part of the picture *Hop to It, Bell Hop, Part II*. These records are from the same section of the picture as the records of Figs. 3 and 5. With allowance made for differences in resistance and differences in the speed of the film, the similarity of the pattern of response is clearly illustrated.

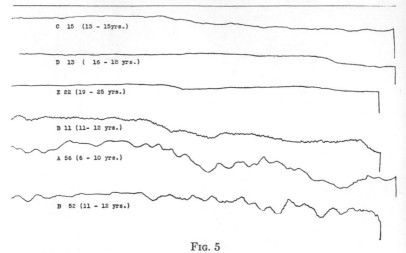

FIG. 5

These tracings of the galvanic record were selected at random for comparison with the records of the reshowing technique, Figs. 3 and 4.

The reshowing of *Hop to It Bell Hop, Part I*, is more nearly parallel to the other cases, as this picture is quite similar to *Hop to It Bell Hop, Part II*. There were two small increases, seven points without change, and two decreases. The increases total one while the decreases total four.

The reshowing technique is interpreted as verifying the main technique of the study, not only by giving considerable decreases in the deflection-index, but by showing a surprising consistency in the pattern of response of each individual to the same picture.

RESHOWING TECHNIQUE TABLES VI—*Continued*

HOP TO IT BELL HOP, PART I

	1	2	3	4	5	6	7	8	9	10	11	12	13
D–13 (Dates)													
2–18–31	X	0	0	0	0	0	1	1	2	0	0	0	0
2–23–31	0*	0	0*	0	0	0*	0	0	0	0	0	0	0

FEAST OF ISHTAR, PART I

	4	7	12	14	25	29	32	34	41	51	57	58	61
B–13 (Dates)													
4–18–31	2	2	2	3	0	5	3	4:4	4	2	0	2	0*
4–21–31	X	X	2	0*	0*	3	1	3	2	2	0	0	0

VERBAL REPORTS

THE verbal reports from the *O*s can not be interpreted in terms of adequate scientific analysis. Only a few *O*s were psychologically trained. Many were too young to make careful analyses. The complexity of the situation and the length of time intervening between periods for report would destroy the value of any effort to keep these comments within the field of scientific observation. The reports were rather conversational, discursive, often full of the "stimulus error," and sometimes lacking in frankness and objectivity. On the other hand, as commentaries they are of the greatest value. Leads for interpretation are offered; insights into the experience are given; and comparative factors are clearly seen between the different age-groups.

Younger *O*s often misunderstood the actual incidents of the story. The devil's costume used in *Hop to It Bell Hop, Part II*, by L in frightening B (12) was reported as a monkey (F, 8–11; F, 15–4; M, 14–10),[30] a fox (M, 9–2), a jackass (M, 13–1), a cat or a dog (F, 12–3). These inadequate perceptions were not very serious since the development of the story remained unaffected.

There were other errors, however, which must have affected the understanding of the story. The bottle of whisky

---

[30] M = male; F = female. Numbers refer to ages in years and months; *i.e.*, 8–11 = 8 yrs., 11 mos.; in connection with a picture title, numbers refer to the reading points, as above.

which climaxes *Hop to It Bell Hop, Part II* (36), became a meaningless bottle of medicine (F, 8–11). A subtitle introduces a "salesgirl who could sell Florida oranges in California" (*Hop to It Bell Hop, Part I*), and her trunks became orange crates to one young *O* (M, 10–11). The girl who backs off the building in *Hop to It Bell Hop, Part II* (31) was pushed off (F, 10–3 and 10–7). The Negro cupid whose arrow awakens the Negro porter to the charms of one of the hotel maids in *Hop to It Bell Hop, Part II* (10), became someone who "shot the nigger" (M, 15–6). The fiery writing of the hand on the wall of the banquet hall in *The Feast of Ishtar, Part II* (73), which announces that "your false gods will not save you," became a match which was lighted, and said "I will save you" (F, 8–11). Certain girls were reported to have picked up a drunken sailor to carry him out (M, 15–6), a report which is remotely related to an incident in the picture in *The Feast of Ishtar, Part II* (between 48 and 59). Tisha was reported to have called Jether a false name (M, 10–9 and F, 12–0), a perception which represented failure to understand the development in *The Feast of Ishtar, Part II* (32). The divine destruction of the wicked city in *The Feast of Ishtar, Part II* (73 ff.) became to these young skeptics a cyclone (F, 10–7), a war (M, 6–4), probably a fire (M, 8–1 and F, 11–2), an earthquake or volcano (M, 13–7), a cloudburst or something of the sort (M, 14–1). The report of the incident of the Negro holding the man and lady in his arms (F, 11–2) is somewhat related to the defense of Tisha by her Negro guards in *The Feast of Ishtar, Part II* (40). "The tricks that the man did to the king" (M, 6–4) was an incorrect report of the Jew's backward reach with twisted arm, a mute request for a tip in *The Feast of Ishtar, Part I* (after 61).

At the close of *The Feast of Ishtar, Part I*, Tisha welcomes Pharis, the sea captain, and they drink together. Tisha's Jewish servant reaches for a reward for his service to Pharis in introducing him to Tisha. Interesting reports on this scene came from young *O*s. The Jewish servant was reported to want some of the wine (M, 11–10 and M, 14–10). Other *O*s felt that Pharis should not drink in front of the girl and that the Jew was objecting (F, 10–11 and F, 12–3). One was not sure whether they were drinking water or what not (M, 14–10).

The love-scenes gave much difficulty among the younger children in the field of perception. Contrasting, for example, with the adult report (M, over 25) that the "clothing enhanced the erotic effect," there were several reports which showed a quite different perception. One young *O* (M, 6–4) thought it was "sad when the girl crept into his lap." Another saw the scenes as an effort of one man to get the girl from the other (F, 11–2) although the story quite clearly shows the girl as the aggressor, and clearly shows her interest in any number of admirers who might have sufficient gold. An even greater contrast is seen in the reports of the love-scene in *The Feast of Ishtar, Part I* (25–41). Quite briefly the glimpse is given of the Jewish servant peering through the drawn curtains at the love-scene. No adults reported the incident and probably no adult would miss the obvious financial purpose in the love-trap for Jether. Yet five children reported the incident as exciting, perceiving the Jew as spying on the lovers (F, 10–7; M, 9–0; M, 10–9; F, 12–0; M, 12–6). While this scene is carried in the general tables as a love-scene, it was doubtless perceived by many of the younger *O*s as a danger-scene. More maturely and yet naïvely, one adolescent *O* reported that "that guy thought that the love-scenes were exciting, all right," although this *O* did not find them so (M, 13–1).

It is clear that among younger *O*s there was considerable confusion in the perception of the incidents which form the story. This is more directly stated by some reports. One young *O* could not "understand whether this one was a friend of the lady, or whether he wasn't" (M, 8–1). The same *O* had trouble in knowing which person was Ishtar (the name of the idol). One girl found parts that "I couldn't understand" (F, 12–0), while a boy, with less frankness, admitted that he couldn't understand at the first although he finally "got onto it" (M, 10–9).

A second general comparison of the perceptual experiences is clear from these reports. There was a wide difference among *O*s in the perception of the artificiality of the picture story. This difference organizes itself clearly into an age-difference.

Among adult *O*s there was a frequent report of a consciousness of artificiality. Once the artificiality of the laboratory showing was mentioned and doubtless it was a factor present to the attention of others. Much more often, the artificiality of the production itself was mentioned, usually as a deterrent to emotion. One *O* was interested in Hardy's acting in *Hop to It Bell Hop* (M, 19–5). The same *O* mentioned the hotel set as unreal and the trunks as empty. Other adult *O*s mentioned the acting technique (M, over 25), the intention of the picture producer (M, over 25), or criticized some phase of the play as such. Disgust with "slap stick" comedy was reported many times in one form or another. The large number of similar pictures which had been seen was mentioned, the whole thing was utterly impossible, or some detail was wrong — as for example, the fact that the four trunks of the salesgirl in *Hop to It Bell Hop, Part I*, all came out of the top of the taxicab which brought them to the hotel. Most of these comments came from the group over 19 years of age.

The references to the artificiality of the motion-picture story which came from children were infrequent, even in the case of *Hop to It Bell Hop,* where the "slap stick" comedy is most evident. One young O (M, 10–9) felt that there was "probably quite a little fake" in this picture, with ten-story jumps without injury and with the fat man jumping clear through the floor. This was a discriminating comment from so young an O in answer to the question about the excitement of the picture. He is a boy with an I.Q. of 145 and his ability to give such a criticism is an evidence of his keenness. No other such comment was offered by children below the 13- to 15-year age-level. In this group, one O (F, 15–4) reported the trunk episode as utterly impossible and later reported the paint episode in *Hop to It Bell Hop, Part II* (4–6), as improbable, since "hotels wouldn't have paint like that around." With a little less assurance a similar question was asked about the lightning in *The Feast of Ishtar, Part II* (75), how the "movies can make that lightning" (F, 13–10); and a boy (M, 13–1) wondered how they can make the walls fall in *The Feast of Ishtar, Part II* (93–94). William Collier, one of the actors, was named in one report (M, 15–11). Yet, in this age-group, such comments were rare as compared with the older groups.

On the other hand, the younger Os assumed the reality of the story convincingly in frequent reports. A careful summary of these reports would mean the reproduction of these numerous comments. A comment concerning the theft of a ring from the hand of a girl at the banquet in *The Feast of Ishtar, Part II* (59) illustrates the point. The "old fellow wasn't drunk—he wanted to be sober so he could steal." Such a comment assumed the story as quite realistic in the mind of this O (M, 11–10). Two youthful

*O*s (M, 8–1 and F, 11–2) wondered how the city was set on fire in *The Feast of Ishtar, Part II*. Another (M, 11–10) wondered how the Jew gambler got out of trouble in *The Feast of Ishtar, Part II* (19–27). Others were disturbed at realistic possibilities in the story: Would Tisha, in *The Feast of Ishtar, Part II*, care for Jether after he had cheated in gambling (F, 14–6)? Would L, in *Hop to It Bell Hop, Part II*, fall from the flagpole while B was shaking it (F, 11–2)? Such illustrations could be gathered from adult reports also but they were neither so frequent nor so typical and were often qualified by a recognition of the artificiality of the production.

The relation of this objective or critical attitude to the intensity of the emotional experiences was often reported by the older *O*s. It was never reported by any child. Youthful *O*s, especially those of 14 or more years of age, may be somewhat critical of the development of the story although this is usually stated in terms of likes or dislikes rather than in terms of the probability of the incidents; yet, in reporting they never approached the amused objectivity with which one college student reported her experience in seeing the destruction of the city in *The Feast of Ishtar, Part II:* "Falling buildings reminded me of fireworks at the state fair—burning of Rome, pasteboard buildings and all—fourth of July" (F, 21–2). Such a report was not only repeated many times in different forms by adult *O*s but was associated with a report of lack of emotional intensity in the response to the picture.

This is the heart of the "adult discount" with which the pictures were viewed. It was also true that some scenes were strong enough with many *O*s of adult years so that the consciousness of this discount was broken down. There were adult reports which assumed the reality of the picture story. Yet the sharp distinction remains between the age-groups. The interpretations of this study are considerably influenced by this fact. The youngest age-group was perceiving so realistically and the adults were perceiving so much more objectively and critically, with the artificiality of the production so clearly in consciousness, that the whole perceptual experience seems to have been different. This is offered as a major factor in the interpretation of age-differences in the intensity of reaction.

A third general phase of the verbal reports is the frequency with which anticipation of possible developments in the story seemed to become a factor in the emotional and perceptual experience. This was true both as a deterrent and as a stimulant to emotion.

Where all of the developments were expected, lack of emotional response was frequently mentioned. One *O* "always had a pretty good idea what was coming next" in *Hop to It Bell Hop, Part I* (F, 20–9); she reported very little excitement and had a very low average response (0.1). Another *O* (F, 17–2) "expected the events in the axe episode" in *Hop to It Bell Hop, Part I* (5) and showed a very slight response until the axe was apparently stuck in B's head, when a deflection of 3 was shown. In *The Feast of Ishtar, Part II*, another *O* knew "everything that was coming," and he gave 14 zero readings out of 19 reading points. Another *O* expected the destruction scenes in *The Feast of Ishtar, Part II*, and his record showed small deflections throughout this series of reading points (6 readings, 2–0, 2–0*, 1–1, and 1–2). Another *O* expected the gambling result in *The Feast of Ishtar, Part II* (M, 24–0), and while the actual gambling showed heavy deflections (4 and 8) the accusations and expulsion gave practically no deflection (0 and 0*). Two other reports like this last one were given by adult Os; the galvanic record for the one is illegible, and for the other is zero. These results can well be compared with the results of the reshowing technique. There, each repetition of the picture showed decreased responses from the Os, with the report often mentioning the knowledge of the outcome as a deterrent to excitement. In *Hop to It Bell Hop, Part II*, two reports gave a similar result. In that picture there are three who fall from the roof of the building. Two Os reported that the falls were not so exciting after the first one (F, 17–5) and (M, 16–9). The former O gave a response of 7 on the first fall, 3 on the second, and 1 on the third. The latter O gave a response of 5 on the first fall, 3 on the second, and 2 on the third. This was not generally true of responses to these three points, however. Other factors enter, such as the girl's fall—the second such incident—and the suspense just before her fall. Yet the third fall showed a considerable decrease in the average of all Os.

The same point is illustrated in the anticipation of complications or exciting developments. When the servant peeped through the curtains in *The Feast of Ishtar, Part I*, one young O (F, 10–7) thought that the peeper might do something. Her response at (29) was 5 and in view of this report must be interpreted as at least in part a response to this anticipation of danger. Doubtless other young Os, who were so much impressed by this spying scene, similarly anticipated developments from the incident. Another youthful O (F, 11–2) felt that it might have meant much when a man tapped another on the shoulder (probably Jew to Jether) in *The Feast of Ishtar, Part I*. When Tisha was given a ring from an unseen admirer behind the curtain in ·*The Feast of Ishtar, Part I* (between 41 and 51), an O (M, 14–1) thought that developments might come from

Jether's jealousy. Other such comments in *The Feast of Ishtar* include the following: whether Jether would go into the room where the sea captain was (M, 16–4); when the captain entered in *The Feast of Ishtar, Part I* (after 61), what would happen then (M, 17–7); when the gods and goddesses were shown (41) there was fear that something was going to happen (M, 12–6); when the old man took the ring in *Part II* (59), there was fear lest something would come (F, 17–5); at least one O (F, 20–0) thought that Jether would return to kill Tisha.

There were similar reports from *Hop to It Bell Hop*. The fair guest's request for a bath towel, together with the changing of the room numbers, led several to anticipate L's invasion of her room, or that "something awful would happen then" (M, 12–6; F, 12–0; M, 25; M, over 25). One girl (F, 10–3) expected the piled trunks in *Part I* to fall from L's back and gave a deflection of 6. Another adult O expected something to happen all the time although his deflections, with one exception, were not large.

In *Hop to It Bell Hop, Part II*, similar reports were given. Two Os thought that B in his fall from the building would hit the street car which had been briefly shown in the picture (M, 9–2; F, 20–9). An adult reported anxiety when the girl was balanced on the edge of the roof in *Part II* (30), and gave a deflection of 14 for that point and the next one combined. It was emotional to one (M, 22–7) to see the actors looking into the hose, waiting for the water to come; tenseness was reported after the dyspeptic jumped out of the window, wondering what would happen next (M, 25); and one child found it exciting to see what sort of a reward there was for L at the end of the picture (M, 9–2). A discriminating comment by one O (F, 19–6) mentioned that there was no excitement when the dyspeptic jumped out of the window in *Hop to It Bell Hop, Part II* (3) since he had fallen before she realized it, giving no suspense.

These three phases of the perceptual experience of the Os combine to give important clues for interpretation. The youngest Os were prone to misinterpret incidents; some of these errors came at points which were essential to the understanding of the story. One may think of such a child perceiving a series of more or less disconnected incidents, or we might find in some cases that the lapses are filled by the child in such a way as to make the result markedly different from the story as seen by an adult. Whatever the child did perceive, however, seemed much more real to him than to the adult. Criticism of the picture was feeble or entirely absent among the young. There was a real "adult discount" which operated for most of the adults. Where anticipation of fearful consequences entered, the emotional intensity was likely to be increased. Where anticipation took the form of predicting the development of the story on the basis of the "adult discount" or on the basis of previous experience with similar pictures, emotional intensity was likely to be decreased.

CHAPTER VI

THEATER RESULTS

CHARLIE CHAN'S CHANCE

(Charlie Chan and Inspector Fife of Scotland Yard are visiting with the proprietor of a Chinese restaurant when a telephone call announces the death of Sir Lionel Grey, a former head of Scotland Yard. The scene of the crime is the office of Mr. Kirk. The doctor pronounces it heart failure. Charlie Chan sees a cat dead in the room; Grey has been working on an important case. These facts combine to pronounce the case one of murder, presumably by gas. A party had been held that evening at Grey's request by Mr. Kirk in his penthouse. The members of this party are given a preliminary examination: Miss Garland, Mr. and Mrs. El, Dunwood, the butler, and Mr. Kirk; the offices are searched; a telephone call to Scotland Yard is made; the safe is searched; Charlie Chan is induced to stay to aid in the solution of the crime. John R. Douglas is discovered to have telephoned Grey before the murder and he is found to be a manufacturer of chemicals. A pearl is found in the ink-well on Grey's desk, implicating Miss Garland who claimed her pearl string had broken on the steps.)

(Miss Marlow calls for John R. Douglas at a restaurant.) She orders only coffee. He reports his visit to Sir Lionel Grey with Sir Lionel's insistence that the girl testify against a former lover and that Miss Marlow's address be given. Douglas had pleaded with him that the girl had suffered too much (1), that it was too much to ask a girl to send a former fiancé to a hangman (2). Much disturbed, Miss Marlow asks to be taken home (3). At the door, mutual professions of love between the two are made with a kiss (4).

(The newspaper story, Douglas's arrest, a letter for Grey, which had been opened and replaced with blank paper holding a thumb print, are shown.) Miss Garland is examined by Chan concerning the pearl necklace. She says the pearl found is not hers (5), but after some urging she agrees to tell (6). She had been protecting a former friend, who is now the masked dancer at the Follies. Chan hastens to leave. The dancer is shown (7) and Chan is seen approaching her dressing room. Chorus girls run up steps near Chan shouting "Chop Suey" (8). Chan is admitted and asks the dancer to remove her mask (9). He accuses her of masking to shield her identity and mentions Douglas's arrest for Grey's murder. She exclaims that he is innocent (10). Douglas's refusal to talk is seen as an effort to shield Miss Marlow. Chan assures her that she can trust him (11) and she tells the story of the London murder by Rawley, her former lover. To his question (12) she replies that she did not escape from London with Rawley. She has never seen him again but believes him to be in New York, since she had seen his Chinese servant, Li Gong. Chan goes to the Chinese restaurant where his friend gives him Li Gong's address.

69

(Chan pretends to fall outside of Li Gong's room. A boy escorts him in and, as a good deed, calls a doctor. Chan asks about Li Gong, has a picture pointed out, is told that Li Gong is a nephew of the Chinaman there and visits the place often. The doctor arrives, discovers nothing wrong with the foot and Chan is curtly dismissed by the Chinaman. Chan returns to police headquarters discouraged.)

Chan and Fife in conference are given a letter by the butler who says that he found it behind the dresser in Grey's room (13). It proves to be the letter missing from the envelope. The thumb print proves to be the butler's (14). It is shown that Grey had been looking for an Englishman named Rawley and the butler might be that man. Chan advises Fife to wait for the arrest (15). It is confusing to Chan.

Miss Marlow, the masked dancer, is seen in costume in her dressing room (16). Asking the maid whether her car is outside, she says that she has decided to tell the police all. A shadow appears, thrown through an unseen window on to the wall. The windows of her car are adjusted and a gas bomb is thrown on to the floor of the back seat by an unseen person (17). The driver is instructed by the maid to hurry away with the note to police and he drives away (18). The car begins to sway, the driver grabs at his throat and smashes into a monument (19). Police push back the crowd, find the driver dead, discover the bomb, and find the name and address of the owner of the car. Again we see the girl in her room in costume (20). The policeman enters and shows the note that had been taken from her car. She suggests that he open the note (21). Asking what this is that she is to tell the police, he takes her away to headquarters.

Detective Flannery examines her. He asks her whether she would recognize Allen Rawley. Hesitating, she replies that she thinks so (22). She is asked to wait in the other room and Douglas is sent for. Douglas denies that he knows Miss Marlow, when she is sent for again. She enters (23) and he denies ever having seen her. She tells Douglas that she has told the police everything. He then tells the police that at the time of his visit to the building to see Grey, he saw a Chinaman there (24). Inspector Fife enters and asks that Miss Marlow be held for Scotland Yard.

(A telephone call tells of the finding of a gas mask in the river. By machine and boat the police hasten to the point, find the tug and the mask, and start the return journey.)

The Chinaman lays a gun down on a table carefully, feels the rays of the sun through a glass, and pulls down the blind. Two other Chinese enter (25) followed soon by Chan (26). Chan is seated in a chair which has been carefully placed. He asks for Li Gong (27). The Chinaman puts up the blind, mentioning that the sun accomplishes many desirable things in this world (28). Chan asks about Li Gong again, is told that the picture previously recognized by Chan is not Li Gong and the Chinaman states, "I am Li Gong" (29). A cat walks over the table on which the gun is lying, moving the gun. In the midst of conversation the gun goes off (30), killing Li Gong instead of Chan. Chan is startled and then picks up the gun (31). A crowd begins to assemble.

(The seller of the gas mask is being examined by Flannery. He sold the mask to a Chinaman. Chan walks in and is identified as the buyer. That ends a promising clue.)

(At the Cosmopolitan Club Chan is trying to identify a number 1313, found among Grey's things. He finds that check numbers run as high as that and discovers that Grey's brief case is checked on that number. He calls Flannery and waits to see who will call for the case. Kirk calls for it and Flannery and Chan accompany him, under suspicion, to his home.)

(At Kirk's home, Inspector Fife is working. Miss Marlow is there. She is asked whether she can identify the butler as Rawley, but she can not do it. An explanation of his mail-tampering is required of the butler.) He replies that the letter from Scotland Yard might refer to an old charge against him and he feared that he might lose his job. An Englishman, who had been present at the Kirk-Grey party, storms into the room,—"You sent for me (32) and here I am." Miss Marlow can not identify him (33). Mr. Kirk enters with Chan and Fife; Miss Marlow has seen Kirk but she is not sure where. Chan shows Grey's brief case and as they are about to examine it, the bell rings. Flannery asks Kirk—under strong suspicion because of the brief case and Miss Marlow's partial identification—to answer the door and pretend that no one else is present (35). He agrees and the detectives step behind doors. Kirk opens the front door (36) and Dunwood (another member of the Kirk-Grey party) enters. He spies the brief case and thanks Kirk for getting it for him (37). Kirk speaks seriously to him, asking whether he would cast suspicion on an old friend. The detectives rush in, Chan's gun pointed at Dunwood. Dunwood exclaims about a terrible mistake (38) and the police accuse Dunwood of being Rawley. He denies it as Miss Marlow identifies him as Rawley. Chan sneezes, dropping his gun. Rawley grabs it (39), confesses the crime, and orders the police out of his way for an escape. Instead, Chan walks straight at him, grabs him, and the other police jump on him (40). The gun was not loaded. Handcuffs are put on Rawley as Douglas and Miss Marlow are seen. Fife agrees to cancel Scotland Yard's request for Miss Marlow and the honors go to Chan.

CHARLIE CHAN'S CHANCE

INTERPRETATION OF TABLES

Miss Marlow and Douglas are talking at the table in a restaurant (1–3). Miss Marlow is greatly distressed as Douglas reports a conversation with Sir Lionel. Each of these reading points gave about the same result. The youngest group showed quite consistent reaction although no large deflections, while the two older groups showed many zeros and few reactions at unity or above.

Words of sympathetic tone are spoken with mention of marriage and removal from the city as Douglas kisses Miss

Marlow good-night (4). Reactions were small but consistent in the two younger groups and quite small among adults.

Chan is examining Miss Garland (5 and 6). The girl is evasive and Chan is stern and aggressive—following her about the room. The element of conflict is real. Adults showed little or no response. The 16-year-old group showed consistent, although small, responses. The youngest group responded without exception in small deflections.

A dancer is shown on the stage as she closes her dance scene (7). The 9-year-old reaction was the largest, with the 16-year group and the adult group following in order. Scantily clothed dancers run past Chan, shouting humorous remarks (8). Deflections were not large and ranged in the order of ages 9, 16, and 22. Chan and Miss Marlow talk in her dressing room (9–12). Her manner is excited and brave. All these points are clearly danger-scenes. The adult reaction was quite small, with 13 zeros from 16 reading points. The 16-year response was larger although there was a significant number of zeros. The 9-year response was more consistent although no extreme response was given.

Chan and Fife discuss the butler's possible implication in the crime (13–15). These are danger-points, though rather mild, and showed a result that is fairly typical of such reading points.

Another picture of the dancer in costume is shown (16). She is in conversation with her maid. Slight reactions were given by all but three of the Os, although there was no very violent reaction.

Danger-incidents are shown (17–19), with the crash of the auto (19). The larger 9-year response, decreasing 16-year response, and smallest 22-year response are typical of such scenes in many pictures.

Another glimpse is given of the dancer in costume (20) with

the policeman approaching her room to report the accident. The response was small.

Miss Marlow and Douglas are being examined by the police (21–24). The larger reactions were from the youngest group, with the largest number of zeros in the older groups. With some exceptions the usual result of such scenes by age-groups was given.

Li Gong attempts to kill Chan and succeeds in killing himself (25–31). The climax is reached at (30), where the gun goes off. There were few zeros in any age-group, with the children showing the largest deflections.

The remainder of the reading points are also scenes of danger as the dénouement is presented. Reaction followed quite closely the age reaction to such scenes. The climax is reached in (39) and (40) as the real murderer is found and captured.

CHARLIE CHAN'S CHANCE

INDIVIDUAL DIFFERENCES

Among the youngest Os there were none who were unresponsive to the scenes of this picture. The smallest response came from N 2 (M), who gave most zero and zero-plus readings. The contrast is widest with N 1 (M) who gave no zero or zero-plus readings. The former boy showed definite reaction at some points, however, giving one extreme reading. The range of difference that appears does not include indifference.

The range of differences at the 16-year age-level is somewhat narrower. All showed some zero responses to reading points and all showed significant reactions to various points of the picture.

The range among the adult group is small. The average deflections were smaller than in the 16-year age-group. Reaction was consistent at other points.

THE YELLOW TICKET

(Maria Kolish is seen teaching in a Jewish school. A little boy comes late, explaining that the Cossacks had posted an order forbidding all Jews to leave the Pale. Conversation makes clear that her father is in prison. School is dismissed and she is seen at home. There is no news from her father. A prisoner returns and describes to the family the terrible conditions in the Russian prison. Maria determines to go to her father to help him in sickness. The home group dramatically appeals to her not to try to go because of the new order but she is determined to go.) At the station she applies for a passport which is sternly refused. She sees a girl with a yellow ticket and discovers upon attempting to buy it that any girl can travel with a yellow ticket, the passport of the prostitute. Maria goes to Madame Rubenstein to get one.

In the Madame's house, Maria is frightened by the scenes of revelry and is asked by Madame to sit down (1) and be unafraid. She gets a yellow ticket. Back at the station she is curtly reminded to report to the police every two weeks (2).

Maria enters the prison gate (3), is searched by the guards, and is led through the great iron gates (4). She asks at the desk for her father and is told to wait. Standing by a window she sees a miserable prisoner tolling a great gong (5), and sees other prisoners walking down a great hole to the prison (6). A guard roughly grabs her with the command to report to the desk. The officer asks whether she wants to take her father with her and she replies hopefully. She is greeted by a chorus of coarse laughter (7). An officer leads her down dark steps to a dungeon door. Maria enters and, after a period of suspense, utters a piercing scream (8). At the officer's desk the death list is checked and it includes the name of Maria's father. Maria returns to the desk and is asked by the officer whether she saw her father (9). Her replies become more and more hysterical until the guards throw her out of the prison (10).

In a court room Maria's name is called (11) and she is sentenced for failure to report to the police. In prison she is roughly ordered to take her clothes off and upon her hesitation the question is shouted at her, "Waiting for a maid?" (12) A physician receives a report that Maria is not practicing her profession and warns her of the brutal life (13). In prison Maria is crying (14) and talking hopelessly with another girl who assures her that she can never get rid of her yellow ticket.

(Baron Andreef enters his office. He refuses to amend many sentences of death and shows much interest in a young woman who passes through his office. He rides with his nephew, a Captain, in the park. A drunken soldier who was caring for the horses had left them, so that he might pay attention to Maria. The Captain protects Maria against the soldier, only to attempt similar advances himself. The Baron follows and protects Maria against the Captain only to insist on her company. The two join a company of army officers seated around a table in the park. She refuses to smoke or drink as the Captain returns with her yellow ticket in his hand. The orchestra is asked to play "The Private, the Captain, and the General," and Maria leaves the table amid coarse laughter.)

(At her old home a letter from Maria tells that she is traveling as a saleslady.

On the train an Englishman, Rolfe, is assigned to Maria's compartment by trainmen who have seen her yellow ticket. He protects her against insult and the two become friends. He is a newspaper man and Maria agrees to give him some real facts about Russian life. After some intervening time, Baron Andreef and his nephew, the Captain, are shown discussing Rolfe's articles which have assumed a new unfriendly tone toward Russia. Maria is shown acting as Rolfe's secretary.) An attractive scene follows in which Rolfe dictates complimentary remarks about his secretary (15). Rolfe asks Maria to marry him and is refused. A kiss follows (16). A servant knocks and tells of a policeman who was looking for Maria.

(The Baron and the Captain are shown in a large public dining hall hoping to see Rolfe and Maria. The latter two enter and sit at a table with British representatives, discussing Rolfe's articles. The Baron and the Captain come to the table and join the conversation. The Baron mentions the articles as especially undesirable in view of recent news, that of war. Rolfe and the British representative leave, the Captain and the British lady dance, leaving Maria alone at the table with the Baron. The Baron remarks that he is sure he has seen her before). She is sure it must be a mistake (17). She tells him that she has been Rolfe's secretary for two months—the time of the unfriendly articles. On the stage, the song and act is "The Private, the Captain, and the General." The two are shown (19), Maria apprehensive and the Baron studying the girl. The memory of the park incidents where the Baron first met Maria dawns on him, he laughs boisterously (20), and says that he now knows where he met her (21). She is deeply disturbed, insists that she will tell Rolfe the whole truth and exclaims about the misery of a girl with a yellow ticket. He replies, "Now, I know the source of Rolfe's information" (22). He professes a desire to befriend her, however, and gives her his card (23) in case the police ever bother her. Rolfe returns and takes Maria home.

(The Captain is seen giving orders to the secret police. Maria and Rolfe are in her apartment. She shows him her yellow ticket. Outside the door a secret service agent is listening. Rolfe insists still that they be married and leaves to return in the morning. The detective knocks, forces admittance, and insists on staying for the night. She shows the Baron's card and he insists on seeing the Baron about it. They leave. At the Baron's palace, Maria discovers through a mirror that she has been tricked. The Baron discusses the articles with her, the necessity of stopping them, and the horrors of the quicksilver mines. Rolfe's card is sent to the Baron. Maria is sent to another room. Rolfe storms about Maria's disappearance. The Baron offers to coöperate in finding her as Rolfe leaves. The Baron returns to Maria and shows her the museum of weapons with which assassins have attempted to kill him. He is called to the telephone and while he discusses plans for putting Rolfe and Maria out of the way, Maria overhears the conversation. She takes a cartridge and a revolver from the museum. The Baron returns, infers that Maria has overheard the remarks, and threatens both Rolfe and her unless she will make the "sacrifice for one she loves.") He pursues her through a door as she runs trembling (24). He crudely approaches, laughing, and she shoots (25) and kills him. Terrified, she drops the gun (26) and takes his key.

On entering her apartment, she finds Rolfe (27). He tells how he avoided the Baron's trap and she tells of the Baron's murder. At the Baron's palace, police identify Maria as the last visitor and hear the command, "Get her" (28). Maria insists that there is no escape for her, not even a trial (29). Rolfe tries to plan an escape. Sirens blow loudly (30); it is not the police, but the call to war. Rolfe finds this their chance for escape and they hurry out of the apartment (31) toward the British embassy. The police car is seen; Rolfe and Maria enter the embassy. An apartment employee tells the police of the telephone call of Rolfe to the British embassy (32) and police follow them. At the embassy the police learn that Rolfe and Maria have gone to the air-field. The chief calls there by telephone. An airplane with whirling propeller is seen (33). The busy ticket-agent takes the receiver off the hook; Rolfe and Maria get their tickets (34); the police chief reaches the ticket-agent as Rolfe and Maria enter the plane (35). The order is given to stop the plane (36) as it pulls out, with soldiers running after it. The two are in the plane, the yellow ticket is torn up and thrown out of the cabin, the final kiss is shown (37).

THE YELLOW TICKET

INTERPRETATION OF TABLES

Maria is frightened at the scenes of revelry at Madame Rubenstein's headquarters (1). The scene is classified as a danger-scene although erotic factors are distinctly present. Three 9-year-old Os showed a small reaction, one gave no deflection, and one reacted quite intensely. All of the 16-year age-group reacted, giving a higher deflection-index in this age-group. The adult group showed the smallest deflections. Maria, using her yellow ticket to travel, receives instructions to report to the police regularly (2). Reactions were all small at this point, with the adult average the largest.

Maria enters the prison gates (3) and a group of ugly prison scenes depict the tragedy of prison life in Russia (4, 5, 6). All Os reacted definitely as she enters the prison, with the greatest contrast between the 16-year group and the 9-year group. During the other prison scenes, the subtle fear for Maria's safety may have been a factor although no such element can be definitely isolated. The tolling of the great gong (5) is the signal of an execution; the large adult

average may be a function of this realization; the subtlety
of such an effect may be diminished by the wretchedness
of the old man who strikes the gong—the reaction might
have been definitely to him. The marching prisoners (6)
more frankly present the despair of prison life. Here, the
youngest group responded with the largest average deflection
and the adult with the smallest.

A chorus of laughter greets Maria's hopeful reply to the
cruel remark of the prison guards (7). The reaction was
small. One might find a perceptual difference in the larger
adult reaction, since the point of the laugh is the execution
of her father. Younger Os must have missed this. It would
be interesting to study such a point in detail to discover the
reality of this possible perceptual difference.

Maria screams (8) as she finds her father's body. Surprisingly small reactions were found at all age-levels. In the
prison office another cruel question is asked (9) and in an-
swering she becomes hysterical (10). Anxiety lest she be
punished may have been an important factor. At any rate,
it is a scene of danger. It gave typical average results with
some variation.

The rough court scene (11) showed surprisingly small
responses from all Os. In jail (12) the attendant speaks
roughly and nude figures are seen rather dimly in the background. Reactions were consistently small. The doctor
warns Maria not to get started in so brutal a life (13). Reactions were small with the exception of two Os in the adult
group (M and F). Maria, in jail, is struggling against tears
(14); she can not get rid of her yellow ticket and fears that
her relatives may learn of it. One 16-year-old girl gave a
large deflection, while adults showed a significant average.

An attractive love-scene is shown (15 and 16). Maria is
clever and winsome in conversation. The incident gave

small but fairly consistent reactions. A kiss follows (16). Each of the 16-year group reacted, half of the 9-year-olds reacted, and a small adult deflection average was given.

Maria is in danger of recognition by the Baron and after recognition is much disturbed by the situation (17–23). The adult response was very small; five of the seven averages were produced by a single O. Only nine zero-plus readings out of 35 reading points were given in this part of the film. The 16-year-old responses were much larger, while the 9-year-old group gave a smaller average again. The potential danger of the situation might not have been so real to the younger Os, especially at (17, 18, 20, and 21).

The climax in the conflict of Maria with the Baron (24) comes when Maria kills him (25, 26). Out of 56 readings from all ages at these points, only one showed no reaction and there were only 11 zero readings, none of which came from the actual shooting (25). The averages show a typical result when scenes of conflict and tragedy are shown. Rolfe and Maria are reunited (27), with both under considerable stress. It is a danger-scene and gave a characteristic result.

A series of extreme readings beginning at this point (28–33) were given by a 9-year female O (Y 7). The 9-year average is heavily weighted by these unusual deflections. No record of movement is found and it is highly improbable that sufficient movements to produce such deflections could have been missed by E. The results are not consistent with the theory of movement of the fingers in the electrodes. No difficulty is apparent with the apparatus, the preceding and the following records being quite normal. A check from the heart-curves is unfortunately impossible, as the pulse records in this case are present on the recording film only in the first part of the picture. The readings are therefore carried in the tables, with the explanation that they come from an O who

	D 1
9 yrs.	
Ave.	.8
Range	0–3
No. cases	6
No. zeros	2
16 yrs.	
Ave.	1.3
Range	0*–4
No. cases	8
No. zeros	0
22 yrs.	
Ave.	.6
Range	0–3
No. cases	5
No. zeros	3

has a considerable number of notations of movement against her record, who shows rather large deflections at other points, and who shows a high heart-rate in the few heart readings. No reliable conclusions can be drawn from such insufficient data, yet there seems to be reason for interpreting the record as an extreme emotion coupled with some movement.

The police begin the search for Maria (28). Without the extreme case cited (Y 7), the 9-year average would be 1.0; all the deflection averages seem low for such a scene. Maria is bewailing her imminent loss of Rolfe and his love (29). Without the extreme case, the 9-year average would be .8; the scene in all age-groups was mildly exciting. Sirens sound (30) soon after the police chase begins, leading doubtless to the usual expectation of the arrival of police, although it is soon explained as the beginning of war. There were few large deflections, although only four of the 19 Os gave a zero reading. Without the extreme case, the 9-year average would be 1.0, with the 16-year average above that and the 22-year average below it. Maria and Rolfe leave her apartment (31). One large deflection weights the 16-year average. In general, the deflection-indices show the characteristic result for scenes of excitement and danger. The police get correct information about the movements of Maria and Rolfe (32). There was little response from this incident, with the exception of the Y 7 case. The airplane propeller is shown whirling (33). Small deflections were given except by the case cited. Rolfe gets his tickets (34). At the 16-year level there was a definite reaction, although other groups gave little response. They get into the plane (35). Responses were much like those at (34). The order to stop the plane (36) gave some response except among the 22-year group. The final escape (37) showed large and consistent responses from all groups, especially those in the youngest class.

THE YELLOW TICKET

INDIVIDUAL DIFFERENCES

In the youngest age-group no outstanding differences were found. Response was given at different points in the picture, but there were none which failed to respond. The only extreme case is discussed elsewhere (Analysis of Tables: points 28–33).

Among the 16-year-old *O*s two records showed very small responses. One *O* (F, Y 16) gave only three integral readings. The other *O* (M, Y 10) gave only four integral responses out of the thirty-seven readings, with eight zero-plus records. The others in this age-class showed much greater response.

Among the adult group, two female *O*s showed small response to most of the scenes (Y 25 and Y 27), while a third female *O* showed consistent and rather large deflections.

THE ROAD TO SINGAPORE

(An officer is posting a notice against the property of Hugh Dawltry. At the club, men discuss Dawltry quite unfavorably. It is noticed that he is returning to India, and Rene, the young sister of Dr. March, shows much interest.)

(On the ship Dawltry is seen at the dining table. He asks about the girl who had been eating at that table and is told that she is eating in her stateroom. He leaves and is seen looking into her room. She is the fair passenger, Philippa. He makes a pretty speech about his cigarette lighter for her benefit, whereupon she slams the window in her room. She lies down on the bed slowly (1).

(Philippa and Hugh disembark at the same port in India. A heavy shower comes up; there is no one to meet Philippa; Hugh in a native conveyance holds an umbrella over Philippa, trying to convince her that she should ride with him.) She bumps into an ugly native, as thunder sounds (2). She accepts a ride with him to the home of Dr. March. As the storm ends, Hugh shields her view with the umbrella in spite of the sunshine.

(The cottage of Dr. George March is shown, with a group of men and women. The doctor rushes in, exclaiming that no one had met Philippa. They ride by automobile toward the ship landing, see liquor being delivered to Dawltry's cottage, and discuss his bad reputation.)

Philippa and Dawltry are shown in a cottage. She smokes and smilingly remarks about his lighter. The two are on the davenport and she recognizes and declines his quiet advances (3). Dawltry tells her that this is his own cottage, not Dr. March's (4). She announces her withdrawal (5) and leaves (6).

(Wedding scenes are shown, as Dr. March and Philippa are being married. The doctor shows his lack of romance. A scene is shown in Dawltry's cottage, with Dawltry drinking and talking about his past in that town and his expulsion from the club. Dawltry hints that he has a new interest in the community.)

Philippa is shown in bed (7) with the other twin bed empty (8). She sighs heavily (9), hears March coming and fixes her hair (10). (March has discovered an interesting case and is quite indifferent to her as he talks about the case. He goes to sleep.)

(An invitation to dinner is shown.) Philippa and Rene are dressing (11). Rene suggests that she will go as she is, to make excitement (12). Philippa rebukes her as cynical (13) and conversation continues. The doctor is heard and is prevented from entering the dressing room as Rene retires behind a screen to finish dressing (14).

(The doctor has found that Dawltry has been invited to dinner. He protests but is not successful in changing the arrangement. A group picture is shown; March is called out; Dawltry enters and has his picture taken with the group in March's place. Dawltry and Philippa dance beautifully together, in contrast with March's awkwardness.)

Dawltry and Philippa are seen on the porch. He rather forcibly kisses her (15) and insists that it was curiosity about him that led to his invitation. She agrees (16) as March comes upon the porch.

(The friendship of Dawltry and Philippa is developing. She is riding early in the morning, to March's disgust. Rene is shown at the club trying to interest Dawltry. Dawltry treats her as a child and declines any affair with her. March must go out of town with a case and cancels a trip with Philippa, taking Rene, however. Philippa is shown receiving and reading a note from Dawltry. March enters and she hides the note.)

As Hugh enters his cottage, he sees Rene reclining on the davenport (17). She likes his Scotch, explores to find where he sleeps (18), and is invited to go home. She refuses and puts her arms around his neck (19). Dawltry picks her up (20) and carries her to the door of his bedroom (21). She struggles and he is amused. Rene leaves somewhat crestfallen (22).

(An invitation is shown from Dawltry to Philippa.) The table is shown in Dawltry's cottage. Rene and March are seen at the boat. March is disappointed because the patient died (23). The cottage scene with Dawltry and Philippa returns (24). An ardent love-scene follows in which the native drums in honor of the goddess of love are heard. Native traditions are told, one of which recounts the experience of a goddess who came to earth to taste sin for one night (25). The conversation ends with a dramatic kiss (26), an avowal of love by Hugh (27), and her reply that she wishes to believe him (28). (They discuss his former affair in the town.)

(Rene and March return to March's cottage. They can not find Philippa.

Rene finds the note from Dawltry, hides it from March, and leaves the room.) She is seen in her own room. March enters and sees her reading the note (29). He grabs it, reads it, and leaves the room. Rene rushes after him and he throws her down (30). He gets his gun (31).

(The cottage is seen again, with conversation between Philippa and Dawltry. An auto pulls up and they realize that it is March.) March knocks (32) and enters (33). Dawltry denies that Philippa is around but Philippa soon walks in (34). Conversation climaxes in her announcement that she is leaving him (35). She declaims against him (36), insisting that any woman would do for him (37). March reproaches Dawltry and there is more declamation. She tells that she is leaving on the morning boat, walks out of the house (38), and drives away in March's machine (39). March on the porch takes his gun (40) and comes into Dawltry's room (41). He announces that he is going to kill Dawltry (42). Dawltry tells him that he has his last chance (43) and walks away while March points the gun (44). Dawltry sets down his lighter and makes a noble resolve (45) as March's arm drops without firing.

THE ROAD TO SINGAPORE

INTERPRETATION OF TABLES

This is a highly sophisticated drama, with subtle points which might be variously interpreted at different age-levels. Such nuances can not be expressed quantitatively but they will be included, so far as possible, in the description of the stimulus.

Philippa lies back in her steamer berth (1). She has just rejected the advances of Dawltry. The incident has suggestive elements in it which may be differently perceived by different age-levels. No large deflection occurred, although the 9-year average is somewhat larger than the 16-year average. Surprise and danger are clearly involved in the collision with the native (2), although the reactions were small.

Dawltry makes advances (3) to give a mild love-scene. Slight responses were given except from two 16-year-old boys, who gave readings of unity or greater. Dawltry tells Philippa that she is not in Dr. March's bungalow but in his own (4), a revelation which was already clear to an understanding O. The social meaning of the situation might easily be lost on younger *O*s. The youngest group gave small responses; the 16-year group gave definite reactions with one exception; the adult group gave slight reactions. Philippa replies that she is leaving (5). Two of the 9-year group gave definite reactions; one gave a slight response. Two of the 16-year group gave slight responses; the other *O*s of the 16-year and the adult groups showed no response. Philippa closes the door behind her (6). One adult *O* gave a large reaction, while no other *O*s gave a significant reading.

The next readings were taken from a bedroom scene. Philippa is in bed (7). Some reaction, chiefly from one girl, was given by the 9-year age-group; the 16-year group gave a consistent response with one large deflection; adults showed slight but consistent responses. The bed of Philippa's husband is empty (8). There was little response. Philippa sighs deeply (9), giving opportunity for various perceptions at different age-levels. The age-order of reaction-intensity was 9, 22, and 16 years. Dr. March, the husband, enters (10) and Philippa fixes her hair. There was a small response except from one in the 16-year group.

Philippa and Rene are dressing, giving a scene that combines conversation with the rather intimate glimpse at the two ladies dressing (11–14). The 9-year group showed substantial deflections, although there were no extreme cases. No direct inference concerning the response of these children to suggestive scenes can be made from such reaction, however, as the scantiness of attire may be also associated with a certain childhood shame. The 16-year age-group gave a smaller response-average, with only one reading of unity in the group. Adults gave almost no reaction.

At her dinner party, Hugh rather forcibly kisses Philippa (15). Two out of the five 9-year group gave responses; all of the 16-year group gave at least slight reactions; one adult showed a considerable response. Philippa is distressed at Dawltry's interpretation of her conduct (16). The scene might vary from a simple incident of distress to a sophisticated acknowledgment of marital unhappiness.

Rene has attempted to capture the affections of Hugh Dawltry. At (17) she is reclining in riding habit on the davenport in Hugh's cottage as he enters. This point, together with (18) which is similar, gave reactions which were quite small. Rene puts her arms about Hugh's neck in an effort to capture the reluctant lover (19). Two 9-year-old Os gave a small response, with three giving no reaction. Two 16-year-old Os showed no response; one gave a slight reaction; two gave definite responses. Two of the four adult Os gave definite reactions. Hugh picks up Rene, carrying her toward his bedroom. Rene resists and shouts (20) to make the incident a struggle-scene; Hugh's evident amusement at her fright decreases the suggestive possibilities of the scene. Both the 9-year and the 16-year group gave definite responses, with one exception in each group. Three of the four adults showed no response, with the other adult responding significantly. Hugh reaches the door to the bedroom; the struggle is more intense on Rene's part and the amusement of Hugh is clearer. The large 9-year response is chiefly the result of one large deflection. In the 16-year group none responded extremely, although there was only one zero reading. Adults gave one large deflection, with three zero readings. Rene leaves his cottage crestfallen (22). Amusing to the adult, the scene may be distressing to the child. Such an interpretation is suggested not only by the scene itself but by the response averages at the three age-levels.

The death of the doctor's patient interrupts his plans for a trip (23). This is a subtle point; it marks the beginning of the dénouement and leads to March's discovery of his wife's

relationship with Hugh. Unfortunately the decisive comment is an announcement of death, to which response may be made definitely by those who can not make the full inference from the incident. This probably explains the large 9-year response, although it does not explain the very small 16-year and adult response.

A cottage scene follows, with Hugh and Philippa (24, 25). The love-making is in part rather to be inferred than seen. At (24) there was no 9-year response, with one small exception; the 16-year response was definite; adults gave no reactions. At (25) there were two 9-year, three 16-year, and one adult deflection-indices. An ardent kiss follows (26). All of the 16-year group reacted definitely; two 9-year Os responded; one adult gave an integral deflection. The 9-year average is about the same as the 16-year, although the latter group was much more consistent in its response. Mutual protestations of love are made (27, 28) and gave little response at any age-level.

The doctor spies Philippa's note from Dawltry which Rene is trying to read secretly (29). He seizes and reads it. The 9-year group showed consistent and definite reactions, while the few cases in the other age-groups showed little response. Rene is thrown down in a struggle with March (30). Response was general in the age-groups. March gets his gun (31). The youngest group showed small but consistent responses; the single 16-year-old O gave a large reaction; no adult out of three cases gave a response.

March is knocking at the door of Dawltry's cottage (32). Consistent 9-year responses were given; larger 16-year reactions were found; the three adult Os gave a slight, a significant, and a zero reading. As March enters the cottage (33), one 9-year-old O gave an extreme response, with the other Os following the pattern of the previous reading point. Philippa faces March in the cottage (34). Child responses were consistent and definite; 16-year responses were consistent and somewhat larger; there was no significant adult response. Philippa announces that she is leaving her husband (35). The 9-year-old Os gave a very large response, with the 16-year-old response smaller and the adult reaction slight. Philippa waxes eloquent (36) as she becomes more angry. There was a small 9-year reaction and practically no reaction among the other age-groups. Similar results were found at the next reading point (37), with the 16-year group giving the largest deflection. Philippa leaves the cottage (38), a scene of conflict. The 16-year age-group showed significant responses, with small reactions from the 9-year-old Os and no responses from the adults. When she drives the automobile away (39), a similar result was given except that the 16-year response was more violent.

March, on the porch, takes out his gun (40). With one exception, the 9-year response was consistent; the 16-year response was larger and showed no exception; the adult reaction was practically nothing. When March enters the room where Dawltry is (41), a similar reaction series was given. March threatens to kill Dawltry (42). Average deflections increased in all age-groups, with the 16-year average the highest, and the adult average the lowest. Dawltry defies March in a sophisticated speech (43), giving responses which were much like those of the preceding reading point, although smaller. Dawltry walks out while March levels his revolver at him (44). Deflection averages increased, with the 16-year group giving the largest deflections followed by the 9-year group and the adult group in that order. Another speech shows March dropping the arm with the gun and Hugh walking out unconcerned. The responses followed in the age-order 9, 16, and 22 years.

THE ROAD TO SINGAPORE

INDIVIDUAL DIFFERENCES

In the youngest group an interesting contrast in response was given. One O (S 2, 10–10) reacted consistently to the love-scenes. There were sixteen reading points so classified; two records were lost through movement on the part of $O;$ five responses were zero; nine were responses of unity or greater. The second O (S 1, 9–10) reacted with two zero-plus deflections and fourteen zeros. The difference in age is probably a factor in this difference also. The other Os in this age-group were girls and gave reactions between these extremes.

The spread is not wide in the 16-year group. Reactions of all Os were positive both to the scenes of love and the danger-scenes. There were less than half as many zero responses at this age-level as at the adult level.

Among adults the range is not a wide one. The number of zero responses was much increased over the 16-year age-group, and they are rather evenly scattered among the various Os. One can detect larger deflections from one of the male Os, but the differences are not so wide. This picture did not arouse much reaction at this age-level.

HIS WOMAN

(Cargo is being loaded on to the ship; an incident occurs which shows the physical prowess of the captain. The captain and mate leave to go to town before the departure of the ship. They part at the door of a saloon which the captain enters. The captain flirts with a dancer; an employee suggests one of the other girls, since the dancer is the boss's girl.)

A small boat ties up at the pier. Sally, the heroine, powders her nose but the boat captain pushes her toward the shore. She protests (1) but the captain complains that she has not paid her fare and hurries her off.

Back at the saloon, a free-for-all brawl is seen, with the captain as the victim (2). The dancer is seen on the balcony as she throws a vase which hits the boss (3). The captain fights valiantly with fists and a chair against many, emerging unhurt. He throws a bottle as the mob tries to follow him out of the door (4).

(Captain rows up to his anchored ship.) As he begins to climb the ship's ladder a baby's cry is heard (5). He picks a bundle out of the rowboat and exposes a baby's face (6). He calls negro porters who follow him and the baby to the cabin. A note is found on the clothes, asking care for the baby, which the captain and the audience read (7). While the captain goes to find a place to leave the baby, the negroes decide to give it a bath. The baby cries lustily as he is put in the basin (8). The captain returns and takes a hand in the bath, resolving to keep the baby. The captain leaves to find a nurse and negroes entertain the baby. One borrows a watch from the other, swinging it lustily and smashing it on the end of the bed (9).

(Sally, the heroine, enters the saloon asking for a letter, money, and a job. She is refused money and a job and is next seen in the steamship office where she overhears the captain and the agent interviewing prospective nurse-girls. Only a decent girl will do, so Sally adjusts her clothes and applies as a missionary's daughter on her way to New York. Her story deceives the captain and she is hired. The captain brings her to the boat where she shows ingenuity in caring for the baby under difficulties. Negroes show Sally to a cabin. The captain speaks to the mate, warning that the girl is to be respected.)

As the negroes leave Sally's cabin, the mate watches and soon enters (10). He insists on recognizing not a missionary's daughter but a prostitute. She refuses the recognition emphatically (11) but the mate promises only postponement. (Sally returns to the care of the baby.)

(Another sailor tells the mate of recognizing Sally. The captain tries to satisfy the baby's need of safety pins by assembling the crew who throw needed pins to him. He gives an emphatic speech about respect for Sally which Sally overhears. An evening scene follows with the fog coming in thick. The captain is on the bridge and Sally comes too.) She says that she does not feel like the same person. The fog becomes thicker and the captain orders half speed. Sally goes to her cabin, taking the baby. The mate enters Sally's cabin (12). He struggles with Sally and tries to silence the baby by covering its head with a pillow (13). The captain hears the baby and soon enters the cabin (14). Seeing the struggle, he orders the mate to his quarters. The mate hisses disrespectful comment about Sally and a fight begins which ends with the mate landing in the sea (15). He is not found. Another steamer is seen right ahead, three whistles are blown (16), and a collision is narrowly averted.

(The ship enters New York harbor and docks. Sally and the captain are to be married. A company representative announces trouble to the captain; Sally and the captain go with him to the officials. Here in the trial group is the mate who accuses the captain of attempted murder in defense of his ship paramour. Discussion centers on the character of Sally who is finally brought in by the captain. Sally, confronted with evidence, confesses her past but the captain is exonerated. He leaves for his ship.)

Sally, following, wants to go with him to the ship but the captain refuses (17). Standing on the outside steps, she dramatically pleads for forgiveness and for one more look at the baby (18). She is refused. She cries that he can rot put the child in an orphanage (19) but the captain calls a sailor to keep her off the ship (20). She leaves crying.

(The captain tries to feed the baby, packs Sally's things, and orders a reluctant porter to take her things to her. The captain calls a sailor to watch the baby, while he goes ashore. The captain meets the mate in a saloon and they drink together. Sally is seen in an apartment with questionable girl friends.) The captain enters the hall (21) bringing the mate to see Sally. She orders them out (22) and becoming more and more hysterical slams the door on them (23). In a violent hysteria she resolves to go with her friends on a wild party.

The baby is shown in the rain, crying. The returning porter picks him up (24) and carries him into the cabin where the sailor guard had fallen asleep. At Sally's apartment, the telephone rings and Sally talks. On ship the captain is seen returning drunk. He sees a stranger on deck and investigates. Sally comes out of the cabin (25). The baby is sick with pneumonia (26) and the doctor announces that there is still a chance (27). The captain stands at the cabin door next morning. Sailing is delayed. He tells a sailor that the baby is not so well (28). The doctor is shown inside the cabin; the baby is shown (29); the doctor announces that the baby will be hungry, that the fever is broken (30); he is out of danger. The captain orders the ship to sail (31) but Sally runs out, wanting to get off. A radiogram is shown—marriage arrangements are made for Sally and the captain, to be performed that day (32). As the whistle blows, Sally nestles close to the captain (33).

HIS WOMAN

INTERPRETATION OF TABLES

The gruff captain treats his feminine passenger rather roughly because of her failure to pay full fare (1). The 9-, 16-, and 22-year averages are in the ratios of 4, 2, and 1 respectively.

A free-for-all brawl is shown (2). Among 9-year-old and 16-year-old Os a consistent and large response was given, with the 16-year average higher through one extreme deflection. Adults showed slight reactions from two out of the four Os.

The brawl continues, with a vase thrown which hits one of the combatants (3). Again large deflections were given by Os of 9 and 16 years of age, with a smaller deflection average among the adults. The fourth point is similar with the adult response larger and the other groups smaller.

The baby is found and is included as a passenger (5–9). To the baby's cry (5) and the exposure of the baby's face (6), the response was quite general in all groups, with averages following the age-order 9, 16, and 22. The appeal is the appeal of the baby in danger and then rescued. The note pinned to the baby (7) gave a consistent response, largest among the 16-year group. The baby's cry (8) gave the same general result that his previous cry gave in (5). The swinging watch which is smashed gave large responses among 16- and 22-year groups, with only one zero reading. The 9-year response was lower but consistent.

The mate makes advances to Sally which are rejected (10–11). The conflict is in the tone of voice and the conversation rather than in any overt act. Both points showed typical conflict reactions by age comparisons. The open attack of the mate follows (12–16). Reactions were extreme from a considerable number of *O*s. The age averages follow the usual order for such scenes,—9-year group the largest, 16-year group somewhat less, and the 22-year group considerably smaller. Four zero readings are found in the last group, one in the 16-year group, and none in the 9-year group.

Sally pleads to see the baby and the captain sternly refuses (17–20). With minor exceptions, typical conflict-reactions were found in these results. The captain and mate come intoxicated to the girls' apartment to see Sally (21–23). The anger of Sally and the open conflict are clear to all. The reactions again were typical, with the exception of smaller responses from the 9-year group at this point (23).

The baby is crying in the rain (24). The scene gave the same general result that the other baby scenes gave. A series of incidents from the sickness of the child is shown

	24	D 25	D 26	D 27	D 28	D 29	D 30	31	32	33
Ave.	1.7	5.0	2.5	1.5	3.0	4.7	5.3	2.5	3.5	2.5
Ran.	0–3	0*–10	0*–5	0*–3	1–5	0*–8	0*–14	0*–5	0–7	0*–5
No.	3	2	2	2	2	3	3	2	2	2
No.	1	0	0	0	0	0	0	0	1	0
Ave.	.6	.4	.6	.4	0	2.0	2.2	1.4	.8	1.0
Ran.	0–1	0–1	0–2	0–1	0–0*	0–6	0–5	0–6	0–2	0*–3
No.	5	5	5	5	5	5	5	5	5	5
No.	2	2	1	3	3	1	1	1	1	0
Ave.	.2	.2	0	0	.6	.2	0	.4	0*	1.0
Ran.	0–1	0–1	0	0–0*	0–2	0–1	0–0*	0–2	0–0*	0–2
No.	5	5	5	5	5	5	5	5	5	5
No.	3	3	5	4	3	4	3	3	2	2

(25–30). Sally defies the captain in returning to the ship to care for the child. Desperate announcements are made of the condition of the child. Unfortunately, the number of 9-year records in legible form drops off at this point to two or three. There are no zeros at any of these points, however, in the 9-year age-group. The general result is again typical.

The final development shows the reconciliation and preparation for the marriage of Sally and the captain (30–33). The scenes are not danger-scenes but share exciting qualities of such scenes. They gave the typical results found in scenes of danger or conflict. The average of all danger-scenes showed the largest response at 9 years, smaller responses at 16 years, and much smaller responses in the adult group.

In using the baby scenes alone, five points are included in which the baby is crying or is quite definitely appealing for sympathy. The average deflection in these scenes, although not classified as danger-scenes, follows the same order. The averages are 1.7, 1.0, .3, for the age-groups 9, 16, and 22 respectively.

HIS WOMAN

INDIVIDUAL DIFFERENCES

No 9-year O failed to respond to the scenes of this picture with substantial deflections. One boy (W 2) gave such extreme and abrupt deflections at the end of the picture that the results are not used in the averages. The curves could have been caused by the movement of the fingers in the electrodes. There is no evidence for this conclusion, however, except in the shape of the curves.

The 16-year group reacted definitely throughout the picture. Some responded with more extreme deflections than others. One girl (W 17) had satisfied her curiosity about the experiment by seeing the picture the day before her appointment. Deflections were quite low in her case, much lower than the others of this group. With the reshowing technique of the laboratory in mind, her response is not used in the average tables. While no record was taken of her first observation, the chances are quite good that her deflection would have been larger upon the first observation.

The range among the 22-year group is also limited. Extreme reactions were few, zero responses were frequent. None departed widely from the usual adult response.

PULSE RECORDS

Pulse records were taken in the theater studies. Figures 6, 7, 8, 9, and 10 illustrate good and doubtful films. The difficulty of identifying the peaks of the heart-curves on the necessarily slowly moving film has destroyed the value of some of these records. There were also practical difficulties in the theater which made accurate adjustment of the delicate penumo-cardiograph troublesome. The pictures were shown on schedule; not all Os arrived at the theater in time to give extra time for adjustments. With the basic study centering in the galvanometer, this instrument took precedence in those cases that gave any difficulty. If the time schedule had been at E's command, many more legible pulse records could have been secured. There are, nevertheless, enough good records to give interesting supplementary data.

The fastest pulse record was read at 154 (average reading). This record came from the picture, *The Yellow Ticket*, from O, Y 11 (M, 16–3). The prison scene (11) was the in-

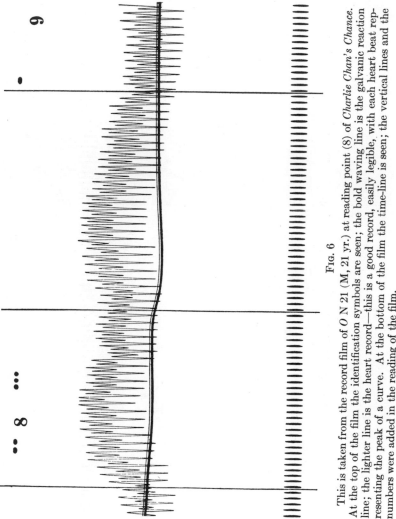

Fig. 6

This is taken from the record film of *O N 21* (M, 21 yr.) at reading point (8) of *Charlie Chan's Chance.* At the top of the film the identification symbols are seen; the bold waving line is the galvanic reaction line; the lighter line is the heart record—this is a good record, easily legible, with each heart beat representing the peak of a curve. At the bottom of the film the time-line is seen; the vertical lines and the numbers were added in the reading of the film.

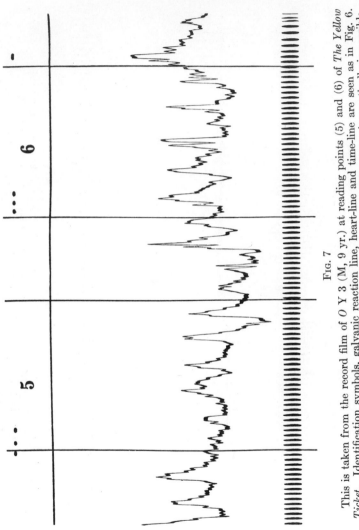

FIG. 7

This is taken from the record film of *O Y 3* (M, 9 yr.) at reading points (5) and (6) of *The Yellow Ticket.* Identification symbols, galvanic reaction line, heart-line and time-line are seen as in Fig. 6. The heart-line is clear enough, yet the identification of the peaks of the curves is practically impossible.

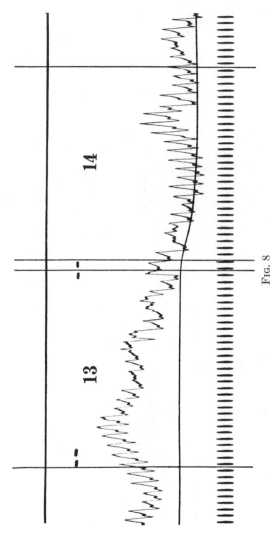

Fig. 8

This is taken from the record film of *O Y* 15 (F, 16 yr.) at reading points (13) and (14) of *The Yellow Ticket*. The heart-record is good except for the short section in the center of this film, where it becomes difficult to read accurately.

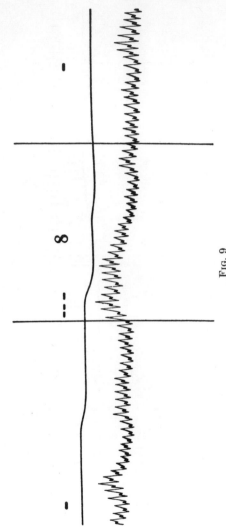

FIG. 9

(For explanation see legend under Fig. 10.)

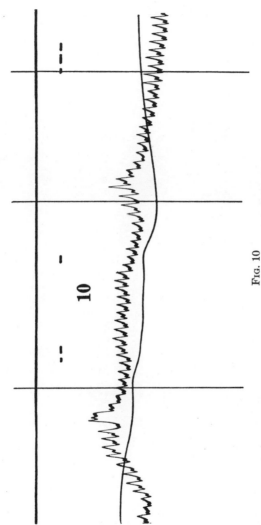

Fig. 10

These figures are from the record film of O Y 17 (F, 16 yr.), Fig. 9 from reading point (8) and Fig. 10 from reading point (10) of *The Yellow Ticket.* The heart-records are easily legible. Especially in Fig. 9, the waves of the heart-line are seen, caused by the movement of breathing.

TABLE XI. CHANGES IN PULSE-RATE

CHARLIE CHAN'S CHANCE

O		Min.	Max.	Range	Diff.	
N	10	80	123	40	(30–31)	123–108
N	12	88	108	20	(5–6)	88–100
N	11	76	96	20	(31–32)	76–92
N	16	80	100	20	(9–10)	88–100
N	17	84	104	20	(19–20)	88–100
N	15	68	100	32	(13–14)	68–84
N	20	60	76	16	(11–12)	72–60
N	21	84	108	24	(17–18)	88–104
N	25	53	100	47	(10–11)	100–76
N	26	72	88	16	(39–40)	76–88
N	1	84	128	44	(5–6)	84–100
N	5	64	96	32	(6–7)	64–88
N	6	74	112	38	(4–5)	74–96

THE YELLOW TICKET

O		Min.	Max.	Range	Diff.	
Y	10	52	88	36	(25–26)	88–60
Y	11	80	154	74	(4–5)	124–144
Y	12	48	88	40	(18–19)	80–68
Y	13	60	80	20	(26–27)	60–72
Y	15	68	104	36	(26–27)	84–100
Y	16	68	88	20	(28–29)	76–68
Y	17	76	104	28	(36–37)	104–80
Y	18	72	100	28	(23–24)	76–100
Y	1	88	112	24	(7–8)	88–100
Y	2	60	120	60	(21–22)	104–120
Y	3	72	140	68	(7–8)	80–96
Y	5	72	120	48	(8–9)	120–100
Y	6	100	120	20		
Y	7	108	136	28	(3–4)	120–136
Y	20	68	112	44	(30–31)	76–100
Y	21	56	68	12	(31–32)	68–60
Y	27	52	80	28	(9–10)	64–52
Y	26	64	104	40	(1–2)	80–64
Y	25	68	92	24	(14–15)	80–68

O column gives the identification symbol of each O
Min. . = minimal reading of each O in the picture
Max. = maximal reading of each O in the picture
Range = maximal change in heart-rate during the observation of the picture
Diff. = largest change from one reading point to the next in the picture

THE ROAD TO SINGAPORE

O		Min.	Max.	Range	Diff.	
S	6	84	120	36	(5–6)	100–120
S	5	89	100	11	(8–9)	96–89
S	2	81	120	39	(9–10)	105–120
S	1	72	84	12	(15–16)	72–80
S	16	81	96	15	(25–26)	96–84
S	10	76	113	37	(38–39)	94–113
S	11	72	99	27	(6–7)	87–76
S	26	51	76	25	(9–10)	60–51
S	20	72	80	8		

HIS WOMAN

O		Min.	Max.	Range	Diff.	
W	1	68	104	36	(8–9)	68–92
W	2	64	92	28	(3–4)	72–92
W	5	76	104	28	(14–15)	76–104
W	6	76	92	16	(3–4)	92–80
W	10	72	104	32	(5–6)	80–92
W	11	80	92	12	(15–16)	84–92
W	12	72	84	12	(22–23)	72–81
W	15	72	102	30	(16–17)	76–100
W	16	80	120	40	(13–14)	100–120
W	20	64	78	14	(26–27)	64–72
W	21	60	76	16	(31–32)	64–76
W	25	80	100	20	(26–27)	84–88
W	26	78	100	22	(14–15)	100–78
W	27	64	88	24	(19–20)	80–71

cident which gave this record. The heart-rate dropped near reading point (15) to 80 and continued under 100 until the climax of the picture, where it reached 120. The lowest reading was 80. The variation in heart-rate was 74.

This was the most extreme change during the showing of the picture. There were many smaller changes, however, clearly indicating that such physiological changes are typical of the motion-picture experience. A table of such changes in heart-rate is appended. The table includes the larger changes from one reading point to the next, together with the maximal change during the exhibition of the film.

CHAPTER VII

AGE DIFFERENCES

Danger-Scenes

This table gives a summary of results from the reading points classified as points of danger or conflict in each of the motion pictures studied, together with the result when such reading points from all of the pictures are combined. The classification of Os in the laboratory by age-groups is as follows: 6 to 12 years, 9-year group; 13 to 18 years, 16-year group; over 19, adult group.

The points of danger were selected from the theater films by E's judgment of the content of the scene; the

TABLE XII. RESPONSES TO SCENES OF DANGER
AND CONFLICT

Picture	No. Pts.	9 Yrs.		16 Yrs.		22 Yrs.	
		Os	Ave.	Os	Ave.	Os	Ave.
Charlie Chan	35	4	1.4	6	.9	4	.6
Yellow Ticket	32	6	1.6	8	1.0	5	.8
Road to Singapore	21	5	1.8	5	2.4	4	.5
His Woman	25	4	3.1	5	2.3	5	1.0
Ave. per pt.			1.9		1.5		.7
Feast I	1	22	1.1	27	1.8	26	1.0
Feast II	17	23	1.7	27	2.1	23	.9
Hop I	13	24	3.2	16	1.9	16	1.2
Hop II	23	20	2.8	13	2.6	16	1.8
Ave. per pt.			2.5		2.3		1.3
Gen. Ave.			2.1		1.8		.9
Iron Mule	20	10	6.0			11	1.1
Gen. Ave. with *Iron Mule*			2.5		1.8		1.0

scenes in the laboratory were checked by two others who agreed that the classification was adequate. Scenes that seemed clearly ambiguous were excluded from this summary, although perceptual differences can be recognized at different age-levels for scenes that are included. The validity of these results is not dependent upon the finality of such a classification, since the inclusion or exclusion of borderline scenes would have changed these results in no essential detail.

That such a classification can be made, however, must not obscure the fact that the table artificially puts results from different scenes together into the same calculation. When the individual tables are averaged and comparisons made with different age-groups, there are differences in perception which affect the intensity of reaction. When these tables of averages are consolidated into summary tables, a highly complex situation is briefly symbolized by the resulting figures.

The results, however, are significant. A real difference in the reaction of different age-levels appears. The difference is consistent from picture to picture. The adult reaction in scenes of danger and conflict is small compared with other age-levels. The 16-year reaction was much greater than the adult reaction average, and the 9-year reaction average was still greater. Whatever differences in the perception of the scenes there may have been, a safe generalization may be drawn as to the intensity of reaction to such scenes. The adult reaction is no criterion of the reaction of younger ages. The reaction is more intense in the latter groups.

The question might be raised as to whether this difference might have been a difference in the mobility of the resistance at different age-levels, rather than a matter of the intensity of the reaction. The question raises the fundamental problem of the interpretation of the galvanic response. This is discussed elsewhere in this monograph. The comparison of the scenes of excitement and the erotic scenes, however, is sufficient to make clear that the result is not a constant matter. In the love-scenes, the 9-year group reacted much less than did the 16-year group.

Another question concerns movement. Might these results be heavily weighted with movement especially among the 9-year group? Movement was checked on the film wherever it was noted by E. That there is some unchecked movement in these records can hardly be questioned, however. This is true especially for the youngest age-group.

Movement unchecked by E would be slight in the great majority of the cases. Much slight movement does not affect the galvanometer. A number of movement symbols were recorded on the record films where there was no deflection. Further, the record in the love-scenes again gives an important check on this item. The tendency of the youngest group was to move more during such scenes than during the more captivating incidents of excitement. The rather small deflections of the 9-year-old Os at such scenes gives the limit to which the most extreme interpretation in terms of movement could go. Further, the discussion of tables showing results of erotic scenes makes clear that there are phases of excitement which creep into the love-scenes. Under such analysis the part played by unobserved movement in these results can not be decisive in the general averages.

The key to the small adult reaction is given in a comparative examination of the verbal reports. Adults are conscious of the artificiality of the film, the quality of the acting, or the probability of the development. Younger Os show a much greater tendency to assume the reality of the picture. This perceptual difference seems definitely related to the difference in emotional response.

LOVE-SCENES

This table gives in summary a comparison of the responses of the three age-groups to scenes of love or suggestiveness. The *O*s in the laboratory are grouped as follows: the 6-to 12-year *O*s in the 9-year group; the 13-to 18-year *O*s in the 16-year group; those over 19 years in the adult group.

The interpretation of the 9-year group average must be made in the light of factors which can not be indicated by table. The classification of unambiguous love-scenes is not so easy as is the classification of danger-scenes. An incident which is itself an amorous scene may be placed in a situation of danger, or may have other such complications. For example, in the picture *Charlie Chan's Chance*, Douglas kisses Miss Marlow and speaks of marriage. This evident amorous scene is a part of the development of the plot, however, which adds the danger-factor. Since children of this age seem to respond so intensely to danger-scenes, this difficulty in classification must be considered in interpreting these tables. Furthermore, the younger *O*s were more restless during the love-scenes, making movement a more important factor. This restless movement is quite impossible to signal adequately to the record film; many small movements of this kind do not measurably affect the galvanic response; many such small movements must have escaped the attention of *E*. These complications reach their maximum in this table with the 9-year age-group.

A more exact statement of this problem carries one to the record films, in order to apply the test of consistency. If some of the young *O*s responded consistently to scenes

TABLE XIII. RESPONSES TO ROMANTIC OR EROTIC SCENES

Picture	No. Pts.	9 Yrs.		16 Yrs.		22 Yrs.	
		Os	Ave.	Os	Ave.	Os	Ave.
Charlie Chan	4	4	1.0	6	.7	4	.4
Yellow Ticket	2	6	.7	8	1.3	5	.5
Road to Singapore	16	5	.7	5	1.0	4	.3
Ave. per pt.			.8		1.0		.3
Feast I	12	22	1.0	27	2.4	26	1.6
Feast II	1	22	1.1	25	2.3	23	1.1
Ave. per pt.			1.0		2.4		1.5
Gen. Ave.			.8		1.5		.8

which are classed as erotic, there can be no reasonable doubt that the response is to the erotic element. This is the result with some of the young Os; there is a definite response and a consistent response to these scenes. With the majority of the Os of this age-group, however, the response is present in only a few of the amorous scenes of a picture.

The conclusion is that the 9-year average in this table must be conservatively interpreted. This is the point at which the complicating factors reach their maximal effectiveness. In comparing the 9-year average with the adult average, these considerations would be important. Where the tables give the general average of each group at the same figure, the intensity of response to the erotic elements was undoubtedly less in the younger group. This qualification is further important since it can fairly be carried over into the table on scenes of danger as the maximal qualification which can reasonably be attributed to movement or ambiguity in those tables; such factors are probably much less effective in the danger-scenes.

At the 16-year age-level, every result of this study combines to show the effectiveness of such stimulation. Reactions are largest in average; they are most often extreme;

verbal reports seldom mention the factors which are termed the "adult discount." Compared with the other groups studied, the 16-year group gives the most extreme response.

The adult response is smaller. This fact is interpreted in terms of the "adult discount." This perceptual tendency may disappear in scenes which are effective enough; yet it is consistent enough to be an important factor in the emotional experience involved in the observation of amorous scenes.

CHAPTER VIII

SEX DIFFERENCES

DANGER-SCENES

THIS table shows sex differences in scenes of danger for all films. The table includes the number of reading points interpreted as danger-scenes, the average deflection of the male and female Os of each age-group and the number of Os included in each average figure. These results are consolidated into scores, weighting the average figure from

TABLE XIV. SEX DIFFERENCES IN SCENES OF DANGER

Picture	No. Pts.	9 Yrs.		16 Yrs.		22 Yrs.	
		F	M	F	M	F	M
Charlie Chan	35	1.3	1.6	.7	1.0	.6	.5
No. Os		(2)	(2)	(3)	(3)	(2)	(2)
Yellow Ticket	32	2.2	1.1	1.0	1.0	.6	.8
No. Os		(3)	(3)	(4)	(4)	(3)	(2)
Road to Singapore	21	1.4	2.1	2.8	2.0	.4	.5
No. Os		(3)	(2)	(2)	(3)	(2)	(2)
His Woman	25	2.4	4.4	1.7	2.6	.9	1.1
No. Os		(2)	(2)	(2)	(3)	(3)	(2)
Ave. per pt.		1.8	2.2	1.4	1.5	.6	.7
Feast I	1	.9	1.3	2.4	1.3	1.4	.6
No. Os.		(9)	(13)	(12)	(15)	(12)	(14)
Feast II	17	1.8	1.7	1.7	2.3	.6	1.1
No. Os		(10)	(13)	(12)	(15)	(11)	(12)
Hop I	13	2.8	3.9	1.7	2.1	.9	1.5
No. Os		(12)	(12)	(9)	(7)	(9)	(7)
Hop II	23	2.6	2.9	2.5	2.8	1.7	1.9
No. Os		(9)	(11)	(6)	(7)	(10)	(6)
Ave. per pt.		2.3	2.9	2.0	2.6	1.2	1.5
Gen. ave.		1.8	2.4	1.6	1.9	.8	1.0

the individual picture by the number of reading points in that picture.

In the theater pictures there are twelve points of comparison in the table. Three of these comparisons show the female average exceeding the male; one point shows the same figure from each group; eight points show the male average exceeding the female. In consolidating the averages, the male response exceeds the female in each age-group. At nine years, there is a considerable difference; at the other age-levels, the difference is slight. The number of Os in the theater study was not large. With this limitation in numbers, only gross differences can be received as significant.

In the laboratory films there are again twelve points of comparison. At three points the female average exceeds the male; at nine points, the male exceeds the female. This result is strikingly similar to the theater result. In consolidating the averages, the male response exceeds the female at each age-level. There are fifty-four reading points included, with a larger number of Os in each group. Such sampling of age-levels gives more confidence in the interpretation of results.

The general average is a consolidation by age-groups of the theater results with the laboratory results. The male average exceeds the female at each age-level. This is interpreted to mean that the intensity of emotional experience in the observation of scenes of danger and conflict was greater on the average among male than among female Os.

LOVE-SCENES

This table gives sex differences in response to amorous scenes for all the films shown. The number of reading points which show amorous scenes, free from complications of conflict, is shown in the first column. The comparison continues by age-groups for each of the sexes and includes the number of Os involved in each result.

In the theater pictures there are nine points of comparison. Four of these comparisons show the female average exceeding the male; four show the male exceeding the female; one gives the same result from each group. The number of Os involved is not large, the number of reading points is 23. The average figures show no gross differences.

In the laboratory pictures there are six points of comparison. Four of them show the female average exceeding the male; two show the male exceeding the female. The number of Os is more satisfactory than in the theater. The average shows the female response greater than the male at each age-level. This is a result of the response in *The Feast of Ishtar, Part I*, where the female response was consistently larger than the male.

TABLE XV. SEX DIFFERENCES IN ROMANTIC OR EROTIC SCENES

Picture	No. Pts.	9 Yrs.		16 Yrs.		22 Yrs.	
		F	M	F	M	F	M
Charlie Chan	4	1.2	.8	.7	.7	.6	.1
No. Os		(2)	(2)	(3)	(3)	(2)	(2)
Yellow Ticket	2	.6	.8	1.0	1.5	.9	0*
No. Os		(3)	(3)	(4)	(4)	(3)	(2)
Road to Singapore	16	.9	.4	.9	1.2	.2	.4
No. Os		(3)	(2)	(2)	(3)	(2)	(2)
Ave. in theater		.9	.5	.9	1.0	.4	.3
Feast I	12	1.2	.8	2.9	1.9	1.9	1.4
No. Os		(9)	(13)	(12)	(15)	(12)	(14)
Feast II	1	1.3	1.0	2.1	2.4	.7	1.5
No. Os		(10)	(12)	(11)	(14)	(11)	(12)
Ave. in laboratory		1.2	.8	2.8	1.9	1.8	1.4
Gen. Ave.		1.0	.7	1.6	1.3	.9	.7

The proper interpretation of this result is important to the question of sex differences in scenes of love. It is surprising, since the feminine rôle is so aggressively played in *The Feast of Ishtar, Part I*, that reports of disgust were not infrequently given. Furthermore, the masculine rôle is strikingly unaggressive, far from the type of lover that is traditionally pictured as appealing to female audiences. The further complication is offered that male Os observed the picture in the presence of E of their own sex while the female Os observed in the presence of E of the opposite sex, howsoever unobtrusive he was during the showing of the picture. One verbal report mentioned this factor. How much importance must be attached to this fact is not apparent from the data. The most significant fact is that the picture *The Feast of Ishtar, Part I,* or the laboratory situation offered a theory of larger female response to love-scenes which was tested in the theater; the theater showings failed to verify the laboratory results. This may be a difference in story content or in the general situation, or in the sampling of Os. This complication leads to the interpretation of the general average with conservatism. If sex differences have been found in scenes of love, they come so strikingly from a single picture that they can hardly be received as a valid general result on the basis of this study.

CHAPTER IX

CONCLUSIONS

1. INDIVIDUALS differed widely in response to the emotional stimulation of the motion picture as measured by the psychologalvanic technique. Such individual differences were found in all of the age-groups.

2. The scenes of pseudo-tragedy, conflict, and danger incited responses of varying degrees of intensity in different age-groups, most intensely under the age of 12 years, somewhat less intensely in those near the age of 16 years, and much less intensely among those over the age of 19 years.

3. In scenes of love and in scenes suggestive of sex, the greatest reaction was produced in the group near 16 years of age; adults gave an average response that was much less intense; children under 12 years of age gave less average response than the adults.

4. The most extreme stimulation by the motion picture seems to center near the age of 16 years, where scenes of conflict often gave the maximal response and where love-scenes and suggestive incidents quite consistently gave the maximal reaction.

5. The age at which definite response to scenes of love or suggestive incidents occurred was found to vary among the children. The study fell below the age-group which consistently showed such response. Most children of 9 gave very little response. At 10, some were found to respond. At 11 and 12, others responded. Above 13, there was usually

110

a definite response. The peak in intensity of reaction does not seem to be reached until the age of 16 years.

6. In estimating the probable effect of a motion picture on a youthful audience, the adult experience during observation is not an adequate basis; since the response of the younger ages is likely to be much more intense in the tragic scenes, and near the age of 16 years much more intense in the amorous scenes. Differences of perception at different age-levels complicate such an effort even further.

7. Wide differences in perception were found in the different age-groups, especially in the comparison of the group under 12 years of age with the adult group. Errors of perception at this age must radically affect the understanding of the story.

8. The adult perception of the artificiality of the pictorial story seemed to be intimately related to the decrease in emotional intensity among Os of this group, just as the absence of this perceptual tendency in the younger age-groups seemed to be related to the larger deflection averages. This factor is termed the "adult discount."

9. Some evidence was gathered to show that anticipation of danger, sometimes based on inaccurate perceptions, became a stimulus to emotional reaction.

10. Adults frequently reported disgust or indifference when "slap stick" comedy was seen on the screen.

11. Upon repeated observation of the same picture, the deflection-index decreased to a marked degree in danger-scenes. This result supports the assumption of the correlation of the psychogalvanic technique with emotional experience and also reënforces the significance of the "adult discount" in its relation to the intensity of the emotion experienced in observing the picture.

12. The male response to danger-scenes exceeded somewhat the female average reaction.

13. There was no clear sex difference in the response to scenes of love or suggestiveness.

14. There were considerable changes in heart-rate during the observation of the motion picture, giving a clue to the considerable physiological change involved in the experience.

15. The use of a continuous stimulus, such as the motion picture, holding O's attention over considerable periods of time, affords an opportunity for laboratory control comparable with the less complex series of discrete stimuli.

CHAPTER X

PRACTICAL CONCLUSIONS AND INFERENCES

THIS study offers a contribution to the practical question of the effect of motion pictures upon developing children and young people. The experimental procedure can contribute little directly to the problems of mental hygiene and morality which seem to be involved. Yet there are practical questions toward the solution of which the study contributes some data.

An important question has been asked: What is the practical meaning of the deflection-indices of the study? The basic answer to the question is comparative, using the adult experience as the criterion in the comparison. Further leads can be given, however. Extreme deflections at the danger-points were comparable with the deflections produced in the laboratory through other researches on fear which we have quoted above. The deflections in response to the amorous scenes are based on fewer records for comparison since it was obviously not possible to carry on extensive research in this direction as was done in the case of fear and similar emotional experiences. A number of preliminary investigations made in this field with suitable observers, however, did reveal deflections comparable with the more extreme results obtained in connection with the amorous scenes in the motion-picture situation. The investigators are convinced, therefore, that the results obtained in the present study in the motion-picture theater are directly comparable

113

to similar situations produced under the conditions of more refined laboratory control.

Furthermore, the results by age-groups showed that adults can not identify their own experience with that of the child. The adult experience seemed to be near the minimum in intensity, influenced by the consciousness of the artificiality of the pictorial presentation.

The question is then raised whether immunity or decreased emotional response results from frequent observation. The surprising difficulty in getting accurate records of attendance from individual children reduces the contribution of this study at this point to the realm of the anecdotal. One *O* was an usher in the theater; another was reliably reported to be in the habit of attending the theater every evening until her mother came home from work. Such *O*s show no evidence of immunity from extreme emotion. Other *O*s whose record of infrequent attendance is reasonably reliable seem to give no unusual response.

The further question has been asked of the authors, "At what ages may children safely begin to attend motion pictures?" So far as the erotic factor is concerned, most children of 9 years have not responded convincingly to such scenes. This study has no technique for isolating any cumulative factor, *e.g.*, whether frequent observation at an age which gives no measurable response would hasten the time when a definite response is made. During the adolescent period, a considerable degree of response to amorous scenes seems to be characteristic. The desirability or undesirability of such a degree of stimulation of the sexual emotions during adolescence is a point on which public opinion, mental hygiene, and ethics may speak with authority.

Scenes of danger and conflict incite strong emotions among children of all age-levels. The question of the desirability of such emotional arousal is a difficult one. The necessity for quiet in the theater seems to be intimately related to the problem. These motion-inciting emotions must be suppressed to a considerable degree. At the extreme, this experience may be considered as questionable for the health of the child. It may be that this is an understatement; yet there is enough disagreement among authorities on the issues that are involved here to indicate that a more positive statement ought to come from the physiologist or the physician, rather than from the psychologist.

Conclusions in the field of social control seem to be too far from the data of the study for the expression of an opinion. One suggestion follows from the evidence of this study, however: The restriction of observation of certain pictures by ages seems to be specifically supported, providing such restriction is made by understanding critics.

It is an undeniable fact, from the data of this study, that there are large individual differences in the emotional reactions to the motion pictures and differences that are traceable to a variety of contents of the plots of these pictures. We are making further studies involving an analysis of the personnel of many of our Os by way of case history and character traits. In advance of this forthcoming study it is difficult and scientifically unreliable to foresee the results. Yet it is clear that in the last analysis attendance at the motion-picture theater is a matter of individual mental lives and must be regulated or at least judged according to the individual psychophysiological organism. Generalizations may be made on the basis of average results, but the question resolves itself into a personal equation: the person who attends the theater in terms of his peculiar mental and physical constitution.

Another important aspect of the problem remains to be

considered. We have noted above the frequent and almost typical tendency on the part of adolescents and children below the adolescent age to note specific incidents and episodes in an isolated manner. The emotional reactions as recorded by our instruments are to specific incidents in the scenes. These incidents correspond to so-called "reading points" which were also recorded by special symbols on the record at the time. But more obvious in this respect were the comments made by the individual subjects. They were largely interested in and moved by the scene of conflict or of danger or of love rather than by the picture as a whole. We might almost state this as an inverse relationship. The younger the child the more he appreciated and emotionally responded to the separate items in the film and the less he appreciated or even assimilated the continuity of the story, to say nothing of the moral or ultimate outcome of the picture.

This outstanding fact is becoming even more evident in the work which we are doing now with abnormal patients. In several of these cases the patients failed to realize that the two reels of a single story belonged together as parts of one story. In *The Feast of Ishtar*, where this occurs, no continuity whatsoever was observed. In many of the films, moreover, there was little or no perception of the final outcome. When in the last scenes an angry Providence wreaks its vengeance on the sinful population through holocaust and destruction they often failed to see the significance of this at all. The discovery of this mental fact is another illustration of the contributions made by abnormal psychology. In the abnormal cases as Bridges so admirably points out, we have a clear over-emphasis of normal conditions.[31] He says, "The distinction between normal individual

---

[31] Bridges, J. W. "Psychology, Normal and Abnormal," D. Appleton & Co., New York, 1930, p. 25 ff.

differences and abnormal variations in personality is wholly arbitrary. . . ."[32] In a similar manner Störring long ago showed that in abnormal cases nature provides experimental evidence which normal psychology does not dare to produce. He says,

"Nothing, therefore, is more natural than that in ascertaining normal *mental* functions, mere observation should again be supplemented not only by experiments which *we* make, but also by experiments which *nature* makes for us, that is, by pathological cases.

Since nature in these cases accomplishes what normal psychology achieves by experiment, the observation of morbid phenomena has in mental pathology the value of experiment in normal psychology."[33]

But we already have pronounced evidence of this effect in our own experiments with children of various ages. The isolated episodes, in other words, repeatedly stood out in attention and in emotion. The story as a whole had little or no effect. This discovery is furthermore in agreement with many of the facts revealed in the genetic psychology of children. Numerous studies have indicated that mind develops from the concrete to the abstract. As experience accumulates, specific incidents become generalized and the power of generalization itself develops. But this can take place only on the basis of repeated events in the life of the individual. It has often been said, for example, that wallpaper is not "paper" at all to the very young child at first but "something which he must not touch," or "something which he must not scratch up." He has not seen it off the wall as "paper" but has simply received these negative injunctions. Abstract ideas and general concepts begin to accumulate only as his experience grows and the power of

[32] *Ibid.* p. 474.
[33] Störring, G. " Mental Pathology and Normal Psychology," trans. by T. Loveday, Sonnenschein, London, 1907, p. 7.

generalization itself develops. Consequently, we have no right to expect that very young children or even adolescents will make the same synthesis of a motion picture that the adult does.

But a more serious consequence of this psychological fact is that many of the claims of the motion picture industry by the same token fall to the ground when these pictures are viewed by very young children, early adolescents, and sometimes even during the late adolescent years. An exciting robbery, an ecstatic love-scene, the behavior of a drunkard, and the like, can not be toned down by the moral situation at the end of the picture when the episode is justified in terms of the hand of the law or the retribution of an outraged Providence. It is not altogether clear, therefore, that the claim made in terms of a mature mind can hold for the growing mind. The ultimate outcome of the story, the moral that honesty is the best policy, the assumption that the way of the sinner is hard, are adult generalizations and belong to what we have called the adult discount. Even if the picture clearly depicts this outcome it very seldom strikes the attention of the younger generation with anything like the force that it does to the adult mind.

But it remains to be said that we must be guided in practice by such generalizations as can safely be drawn from average scientific results. Otherwise generalizations will be made on the basis of much slimmer facts or no facts at all. It also remains to be said that the moving and talking pictures are a powerful stimulus, especially at certain ages and notably at the pre-adult ages, to conduct and behavior. Then, too, there is less convention (and no tradition) surrounding this art than there is about the so-called legitimate theater, with its vast background of custom and popular acquiescence. When the pictures are finally shown in color, as they undoubtedly will soon be quite generally shown, and when the stereoscopic effect of tridimensional perception is added, which is also possible within a decade, an irresistible presentation of reality will be consummated. Even as they are now, however, the moving and talking pictures in their present vogue carry a tremendous sanction. When, therefore, a psychoneurotic adolescent, for example, is allowed frequently to attend scenes depicting amorous and sometimes questionably romantic episodes, the resultant effects on that individual's character and development can be nothing but baneful and deplorable. From this extreme example there are, of course, all varieties of deviation with modified attending influences.

Our records are clear on this point: profound mental and physiological effects of an emotional order are produced. The stimulus is inherently strong and undiluted by post-adolescent critical attitudes and accumulated and modifying experiences. Unnatural sophistication and premature bodily stimulation will then result. The emotions are widely known in the psychological literature for their extensive and intensive grip on mind and body. Let those moralize and standardize who will: our fundamental facts speak loudly for themselves.

INDEX

Adult discount, 62 f., 64 f., 68, 105, 111

Age differences, 1, 3, 4, 6, 11, 12, 13, 22–26, 28–31, 32–40, 42–50, 59–68, 71–73, 76–80, 82–87, 89–92, 100–105, 106, 110, 111, 114, 115–119

Ambiguous scenes, 41 f., 43, 45

Analysis of motion pictures, 15, 17

Apparatus, 13 ff.; schematic drawing, 19

Bayley, 9, 10

Bertholon, 7

Calibration of instrument, 11, 19

Charlie Chan's Chance, story of film, 69 ff.; interpretation of tables, 71 ff.; summary tables, insert, 72; individual differences, 73

Classification of scenes, 100 f.

Conclusions, 110 ff.

Conflict-scenes, *see* Danger-scenes

Danger-scenes, 21–31, 37, 41–48, 69–73, 74–79, 80–87, 87–92, 106 f., 110, 112; general table, 100

Darrow, 9

Dysinger, D. W., 9, 10

Eastman kodascope, 13

Erotic scenes, 31–41, 42, 43, 45, 61, 69–73, 74–79, 80–87, 103 ff., 107 ff., 110, 112; general table, 104

Feast of Ishtar, Part I, story of film, 31 ff.; summary tables, 32 ff.; interpretation of tables, 35 ff.; individual differences, 38 ff.; sex differences, 40 f.; Part II, story of film, 41 ff.; summary tables, 42 f.; interpretation of tables, 44 ff.; individual differences, 46 f.; sex differences, 47 f.

Féré, 8

Frequency of attendance at theater, 114

Gildemeister, 9

Heart-records, *see* Pulse-rate

His Woman, story of film, 87 ff.; interpretation of tables, 89 ff.; summary table, insert, 90; baby-scenes, 91; individual differences, 91 f.

Hop to It, Bell Hop, Part I, story of film, 21 f.; summary tables, 22 ff.; interpretation of tables, 25; individual differences, 25 f.; sex differences, 26; Part II, story of film, 27 ff.; summary tables, 28 f.; interpretation of tables, 30; individual differences, 30 f.; sex differences, 31

Index of deflection, 11, 113

Individual differences, 25 f., 30 f., 38 ff., 46 f., 73, 80, 87, 91 f., 110, 115, 118 f.

Iron Mule, summary tables, 48 f.; story of film, 49; interpretation of tables, 50

Laboratory studies, *see Feast of Ishtar, Hop to It, Bell Hop, Iron Mule*

Landis, 9

Love-scenes, *see* Erotic scenes

Mental hygiene, 3, 114, 115

Motion picture as laboratory method, 10, 112

Movement of observers, 102, 104

Müller, 8

Observers, 12 f., 16

Patterson, 9, 10

Perception of continuity, 115 f.

Perceptual differences, 3 f., 59 ff., 68, 111; artificiality of motion picture, 62 ff., 111; anticipation of development, 65 ff., 111

Pneumo-cardiograph, 14 f.; *see also* Pulse-rate

121